THE
CAR

BOOK

Haynes

THE
BOOK ®

Contents

Making the most of your car

The average privately owned car has to be many things in the course of a year: commuter vehicle, school bus, shopping trolley, tow truck and holiday transport. This chapter looks at how your car can fulfil all these roles without costing you a fortune. Besides some of the more obvious ways of saving money on running costs, there are tips on how to avoid unwelcome bills in the first place and how to minimise the expense and inconvenience of a breakdown. There's also advice on security (yours and the car's), and on carrying children and unusual loads.

Things you should always carry

It's a good idea to keep a few items in your boot to get you out of trouble if you're unfortunate enough to have a problem during a journey. It's worth noting that in some countries, it's compulsory to carry certain items, such as a warning triangle, first aid kit and spare light bulbs.

The basic tool kit supplied with your car won't allow you to do much more than change a wheel! It's a good idea to carry a few extra basic tools just in case – even if you can't fix a problem yourself, someone else might be able to help if you can supply a screwdriver.

Warning triangle (may be compulsory)

Spare alternator drivebelt

Roll of insulating tape

Wheel brace with extending handle

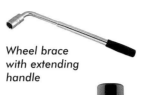
Windscreen de-icer spray (in winter)

Coil of stout wire

Selection of hose clips

Emergency kit and spares

Here's a selection of items and spares which you might want to carry – the list could be endless, but it's a question of striking a balance between taking up space and having the necessary item to get you out of trouble.

Spark plug, properly cleaned and gapped (petrol engine cars)

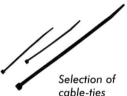

Spare fuses (10, 20 and 30 amp)

Coolant hose repair bandage

Fire extinguisher (may be compulsory)

Set of spare light bulbs (may be compulsory)

Selection of cable-ties

Luggage elastic "bungee"

Tools

Here are some tools which won't take up much space, and will help to fix simple problems at the roadside. If you decide to carry out DIY maintenance, you'll need these tools anyway – refer to "Tools" for more information.

Can of water-dispersant spray

First aid kit (may be compulsory)

Ignition HT lead, to reach spark plug furthest from distributor/coil (petrol engine cars)

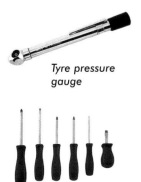
Tyre pressure gauge

A wad of clean cloth

Pliers

Spanners, or basic socket set (covering range 10 to 19 mm)

Screwdrivers (flat-blade and crosshead)

Torch

Spark plug spanner and gapping tool (petrol engines)

Documentation

In some countries it's compulsory to carry your vehicle documentation with you at all times (driving licence, certificate of insurance, vehicle registration document and vehicle test certificate), and you should do this in any case if you're travelling abroad. But remember not to leave them in the car.

How to save money

For most people, apart from looking after a family and running a home, owning a car is probably the biggest single source of expense!

If you work it out, the total cost of running a car for a year (fuel, insurance, servicing, road tax, depreciation, etc) can be frightening. There are lots of areas where you can easily make economies, or at least avoid spending money unnecessarily. Here are a few helpful hints.

Fuel

For the majority of people, by far the biggest expense involved in running a car is the cost of fuel. If you've got into the habit of filling your car with fuel regularly, have you stopped to work out how much it's costing you over a year? This is worth thinking about when you're considering replacing your car.

Depending on where you live; "own-brand" supermarket fuel may be significantly cheaper than branded fuel from a garage or service station. It may also be more convenient for you to fill up when you do your shopping. The oil companies will argue that their own branded fuels contain beneficial additives which aren't necessarily included in supermarket fuel. There's no definite answer to the question of whether the branded fuels are worth the extra cost, but it's true to say that supermarket fuel meets the appropriate national standards and you certainly won't cause any serious damage to your car by using it.

The car itself

First, there's the choice between petrol and diesel engines. Diesel engines are generally more economical than petrol engines, and modern diesel engines are every bit as powerful as their petrol counterparts.

Secondly, the smaller the car, the smaller the engine needs to be, and the more economical it's going to be – however, even if you're stuck with a seven-litre turbocharged monster, there are still ways to reduce running costs.

Maintenance

A well-maintained car will always be more economical than a similar poorly-maintained example, and we're not just talking about engine maintenance. For instance, if the tyre pressures are too low, this will create more friction between the tyre and the road, and so fuel consumption will increase. (Don't, however, increase your tyre pressures above the manufacturer's recommendations in an attempt to save fuel!) Similarly, if the brakes are poorly maintained, they may drag, again creating more friction than necessary. So skimping on maintenance is going to cost you money in the long run.

DIY maintenance

Have you considered carrying out DIY maintenance on your car? The cost of an hour's labour at a garage will pay for at least one tankful of fuel for most cars! Even if you only do the simpler jobs like changing the oil and filter, you can make a worthwhile saving. Details of the basics checks are given in "Fluids and filters", but if you're keen to learn more about how your car works, then a car maintenance course or an evening class at college, will give you a more detailed picture.

Driving style

The biggest influence on fuel consumption is driving style. Basically, the smoother the driving style, the more economical it will be. You'll also find that fuel consumption increases rapidly when the cruising speed goes up.

Insurance

It's always worth shopping around for quotes from different companies (but make sure the policies you're comparing are similar).

You can often reduce the cost by increasing your voluntary excess. This means that you will have to pay more if you make a claim, but your annual premium will be lower.

Savings can also be made by restricting the cover. It may not be worth insuring an older car with comprehensive cover, and inexperienced drivers on your policy will also push the cost up. Some insurance companies will also give a discount to members of motoring clubs, or if you have a security device fitted. Refer to "Car insurance" for more information.

Depreciation

It's not until you decide to sell your car, or trade it in for a newer model, that you find out just how much money you've lost through depreciation since you bought it! The biggest amount of depreciation usually takes place in the first year of a car's life. If you buy a year-old car from a reputable dealer it will have a similar guarantee to a brand-new model, but someone else will have paid for that first-year depreciation.

Obviously, mileage has a big effect on depreciation, but there may not be much you can do to reduce the mileage you cover. Apart from mileage, the two main factors are the car's condition, and service history.

The law

Speeding tickets and parking fines can prove very costly. As far as driving and the law are concerned, if you break the law, you must expect to pay the penalty.

Do you need to use your car?

On short journeys (anything much under 10 minutes), the engine won't reach its normal working temperature, and fuel consumption (and engine wear) will be significantly higher than usual.

If you work close to your home, could you walk or cycle to work, or use public transport? You might even find it quicker than driving.

If you don't need a car to do your job, public transport could prove more convenient than driving, as well as cheaper, and far less stressful.

Other factors

Sometimes other factors increase fuel consumption, even though you haven't changed your driving style.
- Sitting in traffic jams
- Towing, or carrying a heavy load
- A roof-rack (increased wind resistance, even empty)
- Frequent short journeys (more fuel is used when the engine is cold)
- Long journeys in strong headwinds
- Long distances driving up or down steep hills
- Abnormally hot or cold weather

TOP TEN MONEY-SAVING TIPS

1 **DON'T** buy a brand-new car; buy year-old or ex-demonstrator.
2 **CHECK** out insurance costs, servicing costs and fuel consumption before buying.
3 **SHOP** around for insurance.
4 **DRIVE** gently. Your fuel bills will be lower, and you'll also avoid wear and tear.
5 **STAGGER** your journey times to avoid traffic jams – if stuck, switch off your engine.
6 **CHECK** tyre pressures regularly. Under-inflated tyres increase fuel consumption.
7 **AVOID** short journeys.
8 **CONSIDER** buying supermarket fuel if it's significantly cheaper.
9 **THINK** about doing at least some of your own maintenance.
10 **STAY** on the right side of the law!

Car security

Car manufacturers are far more aware of car security these days, and many cars are supplied with etched window glass, immobilisers, alarms and protected in-car entertainment equipment as standard. Apart from fitting security devices, there are several common-sense steps you can take to make life harder for would-be criminals. Some of the points might seem obvious, but the majority of cars are broken into or stolen in a very short space of time, with little force or effort required.

ALWAYS LOCK YOUR CAR – even in the garage or driveway at home, or if you've just filled up with fuel and you're popping into the kiosk to pay. Many modern cars have anti-theft deadlocks – if your car has them, make sure you always activate them as a matter of course when locking your car. Don't forget to lock the fuel filler, and if the car is in the garage, lock the garage. If your car is stolen or broken into while it's unlocked, your insurance company may not pay for the loss or damage.

PUT YOUR RADIO AERIAL DOWN WHEN PARKING – alternatively, you can have a telescopic aerial replaced with a less vulnerable flexible rubber one.

PROTECT IN-CAR ENTERTAINMENT EQUIPMENT – most modern equipment is security-coded, and won't work if it's disconnected from the battery.

FIT AN IMMOBILISER – electronic immobilisers will prevent the engine from being started, and mechanical devices, such as steering wheel and gear lever locks can act as a visible deterrent.

NEVER LEAVE VALUABLE ITEMS ON DISPLAY – if you can't take it with you, lock it in the boot. Don't leave valuable items in the glovebox. Don't leave your vehicle documents in the car, as they could help a thief to sell it.

CLOSE ALL THE WINDOWS AND THE SUNROOF – if a window or sunroof is open, you're making the job of a professional thief much easier. A door can be opened much more quickly with the aid of an open window.

FIT AN ALARM – the best alarms are expensive, but they will deter thieves. Many have built-in immobilisers; it's even possible to fit a tracking system which will allow the police to monitor the movement of a stolen car. If you have an alarm, make sure you switch it on even if you're only leaving the car for a few minutes.

PARK IN A VISIBLE LOCATION – if possible, always try to park in an attended car park, and in a space where your car is highly visible. If you have to park at night, in a car park or at the roadside, try to pick a well-lit area (under a street light for instance).

ALWAYS REMOVE THE IGNITION KEY – even in the garage or driveway at home.

FIT WHEEL NUTS OR BOLTS WHICH NEED A KEY – if your car is fitted with expensive wheels. Alloy wheels are easy to sell, and are favourite targets for thieves.

Have your car windows etched with the registration number or Vehicle Identification Number – this will help to trace your car if it's stolen and the thieves try to change its identity. Other glass components such as sunroofs and headlights can also be etched if desired. Many garages and glass specialists can provide this service.

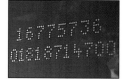

Carrying children

Most parents strap their children into child car seats, confident that they've done everything possible to protect their loved-ones. However, many young children are travelling in car seats which have been badly fitted, or are being incorrectly used, making them potentially dangerous should they be involved in an accident.

NEVER allow children to travel in a car unrestrained – even for the shortest of journeys.

NEVER carry a child on an adult's lap or in an adult's arms – you may feel that your baby is safer in your arms, but this isn't the case.

NEVER rely solely on an adult seat belt to restrain a child – and always use an approved booster cushion to enable a seat belt to fit properly.

ALWAYS strap young children into a properly-designed child car seat.

Choosing a child car seat

Although age ranges are often given by the seat manufacturers, these are only a rough guide. It's the weight of the child which is important - a smaller-than-average baby can use a baby car seat for longer than a heavy baby of the same age.

Never buy a second-hand child seat. Often, a second-hand seat is sold without instructions, and parts may be missing. This often leads to second-hand seats being incorrectly fitted or dangerous to use.

Your baby's first contact with the outside world is often on that first ride home from hospital, so make sure that you're prepared, and buy a baby seat before your baby is born.

These first car seats are light and easy to carry with a handle - this allows a sleeping baby to be carried from the car without waking.

All seats for babies up to around 9kg are rearward facing - this can improve safety, as the baby is supported across the back rather than purely by the harness, if the car suffers a frontal impact.

Forward facing seats, for when a child can sit unaided, use the car's seat belts to hold both the seat and child - make sure that this type of seat is fitted with a seat belt lock, so that the seat belt can't be pulled out of place or slackened.

Choose a seat which has an easily adjustable harness - this will ensure that the harness fits the child securely for each trip, and also makes getting a struggling child in and out easier.

WARNING

NEVER fit a child seat to the front passenger seat of a car equipped with a passenger air bag - if an air bag is activated, it can cause serious injury.

Car sickness

All you can do as a driver is try to drive smoothly, and provide a comfortable ride. Make sure that it isn't too stuffy inside the car (turn the heater down if necessary) and, if possible, leave a window (or the sunroof) open to allow fresh air into the car.

There are several forms of medication available to combat car sickness, but you should always read the instructions - if you're planning to give medication to a young child, it's vital to check that it's suitable. Don't exceed the recommended dosage.

Keeping a child amused

Young children need to be kept amused when travelling in a car, so make sure they have a toy or two that they can play with without distracting the driver.

Carrying heavy loads

Occasionally, you may want to use your car to carry a heavy or unusual load. Before you do, here are a few things to consider. Can you have the load delivered? Can you borrow or hire a pick-up or a van? If you have to use your car, can you make several trips?

Roof racks

Some roof racks claim to be "universal", while others are tailor-made for a particular model of car. On some cars, you may have no option but to use the car manufacturer's own roof rails or rack.

Many manufacturers produce complete luggage carrying systems, with roof rails, and compatible luggage trays, cycle carriers, etc. Often, you can buy a basic set of roof rails, or a rack, with a separate mounting adapter kit to fit your car – this means you'll still be able to use the unit if you change your car, you just buy the appropriate adapter kit.

Rails and racks
Rails fit into tracks running the length of the roof. You can then buy adjustable racks that fix easily onto the rails.

Top box
These come in various sizes. Their aerodynamic shape helps to keep down wind resistance, and most can be locked.

Ski box
This type of top box is handy for carrying equipment for any sport that has awkwardly shaped accessories.

Carrying bikes
Putting bikes on the car roof is another alternative to carrying them on the rear-mounted carrier.

Using a roof rack

If you're going to use a roof rack, make sure that it's correctly fitted to the car.

Next, you need to make sure you load the roof rack sensibly. You'll usually find a maximum roof rack load specified in your car's handbook – don't exceed it!

Even an empty roof rack can cause about a 10% increase in fuel consumption, and if you load up a roof rack without thinking, it can be even worse – ideally you're aiming for the minimum possible amount of wind resistance.

Before you put anything on the roof rack, spread a large sheet of plastic or a tarpaulin over the rack (make sure that it's big enough to wrap completely around the load).

Load the roof rack with the largest items at the rear, and the smallest items at the front.

Wrap the plastic or tarpaulin around the load, trying to arrange the overlap so that the wind won't catch it. Secure it with suitable tie-downs (use the self-locking type with a metal buckle), rope, or elastic cords – an "octopus"-style load bungee is ideal.

Make sure the roof rack and load are secure – give them a good pull in all directions before setting off, and if necessary, add additional securing straps. Remember the load must be secured against sliding sideways, backwards and forwards.

Once you set off on your journey, stop after the first few miles to check that nothing's been moved or loosened by the movement and wind.

Carrying long loads

If you have to carry an unusually long load, the best place to put it is on a roof rack – make sure the load is properly secured, and can't slide forwards or backwards.

If you can't put the load on a roof rack, fold down the rear seats (if possible), and slide the load in beside the front passenger seat – you may be able to fold or recline the seat to give more room. Make sure the load is secure, and doesn't interfere with the driver's controls. If you can't fully close the boot lid or tailgate, make sure it's held securely with rope or a tie-down, and make sure that the number plate and rear lights are still visible.

On cars with a sunroof it's sometimes possible to carry ladders or planks poking out through the opened roof. If you use this method, make sure that the load is secured against sliding into the driver on bends.

WARNING

Anything extending more than 0.3m beyond the car's rear bumper should have a prominent red flag attached to it.

If you can't load the car through the boot, slide the load through a back window, and rest it beside the front passenger seat. NEVER slide a load through a front window, with the load facing forwards.

Safety

Before you start loading the car, consider the safety (and legal) implications.

LOAD the car sensibly – how many cars have you seen driving back from the ferry port full of "duty-free", with the rear suspension on the bump stops and the headlights pointing at the sky? If the suspension can't do its job it's dangerous, and it's also likely to cause damage to the car. Make sure your headlight beams are adjusted to compensate for any load.

NEVER exceed the "maximum gross vehicle weight" - this will be given in your car's handbook.

MAKE sure that the load doesn't affect your visibility – if you can't see through the back window, make sure that your door mirrors are adjusted so you can still see behind you. Never allow anything to hang down over the windscreen.

INCREASE your tyre pressures when carrying a heavy load – consult your car's handbook for details. You may need to inflate your tyres to the "full-load" pressures.

MAKE sure that your car's rear number plate and lights are visible – it's against the law to drive with a number plate or light obscured, and it's dangerous.

Cycle carriers

There's a wide range of specialist cycle carriers available. Which system suits you best is very much down to personal choice – but if you opt for a cycle carrier which fits on the rear of the car, you'll still be able to use a roof rack.

Something to bear in mind if you use a rear-mounted carrier is that you must still be able to read the car's rear number plate and see all the rear lights. You'll probably have to buy an additional rear number plate, and you may even have to fit a set of lights (make sure that they're correctly wired).

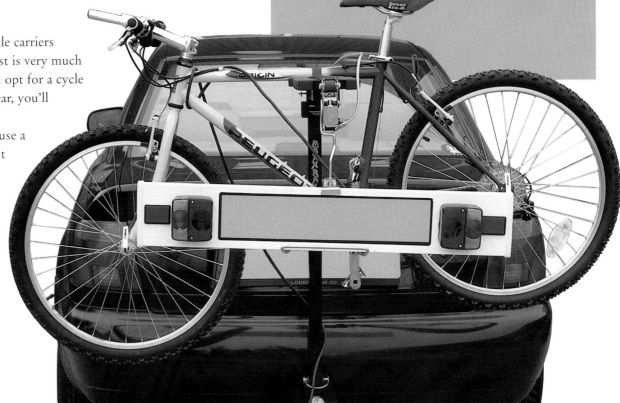

Towing

If you're towing for the first time, there are a few points to bear in mind. First, make sure you have a tow bar which is up to the job! If you can afford it, it's worth paying for a professional installation.

Make sure you're familiar with any laws which apply, especially if you're travelling abroad. In particular, make sure you know the speed limits. In some countries you need a separate warning light fitted in the car to show that the trailer/caravan direction indicator lights are working.

Driving tips

AVOID DRIVING WITH AN UNLADEN CAR AND A LOADED TRAILER/CARAVAN – the uneven weight distribution will make the car unstable.

ALWAYS DRIVE AT A SAFE SPEED – always reduce speed in bad weather and high winds – especially when driving downhill. If there are any signs of "snaking", slow down immediately but gently – never try accelerating, and don't brake hard either.

ALWAYS BRAKE IN GOOD TIME – if the trailer/caravan has brakes, apply the brakes gently at first, then firmly. This will prevent the trailer/caravan wheels from locking. If the car has a manual transmission, change before going down a steep hill (the engine will act as a brake), and on cars with automatic transmission, select "2" or "1" in the case of very steep hills.

DON'T USE A LOWER GEAR UNNECESSARILY – stay in as high a gear as possible, to keep the engine revs low, but don't let the engine labour. This helps to avoid engine overheating.

MAKE SURE YOU KNOW HOW TO REVERSE – this can be tricky if you've never done it before.

Before starting a journey

MAKE SURE YOUR CAR CAN COPE WITH THE LOAD – are the engine, brakes, tyres and suspension up to the job?

DON'T EXCEED THE MAXIMUM TRAILER OR TOW BAR WEIGHTS FOR THE CAR – check your car's handbook for details.

MAKE SURE YOU CAN SEE BEHIND THE TRAILER/CARAVAN – using the car's mirrors. Extending side mirrors can be fitted to most cars.

MAKE SURE THE TYRE PRESSURES ARE CORRECT – unless you're towing a light, unladen trailer, the car tyres should be inflated to the "full load" pressures (check your car's handbook). Check the trailer/caravan tyre pressures are correct too.

MAKE SURE THE HEADLIGHTS ARE SET CORRECTLY – check the aim with the trailer/caravan attached, and have it adjusted if necessary. Many cars have an adjuster on the dashboard.

MAKE SURE THE TRAILER/CARAVAN LIGHTS WORK CORRECTLY – the extra load on the flasher circuit may cause the indicators to flash too slowly, so you may need a "heavy duty" flasher unit.

MAKE SURE THAT THE TRAILER/CARAVAN IS CORRECTLY LOADED – refer to the manufacturer's recommendations. As a general rule, distribute the weight with the heaviest items as near as possible to the trailer/caravan axle. Secure all heavy items so they can't move. Car manufacturers usually specify an optimum noseweight for a trailer/caravan when loaded. If necessary, move the load to get as close as possible to the recommended noseweight. Don't exceed the recommended noseweight.

ENGINE – Don't put unnecessary strain on the engine by trying to tow a very heavy load. The extra load on an engine when towing may mean that the cooling system is no longer adequate – you may be able to have modified cooling system components (a larger radiator, etc) fitted to cope with this if you tow regularly.

SUSPENSION – Towing puts extra strain on a car's suspension components, and can affect the handling of a car. Heavy duty rear suspension components are available for most cars to cope with towing.

Accessories

Fitting accessories to your car enables you to tailor the car to your exact needs, and will give it a touch of individuality. There are a vast number of products available, and car accessories are a big business.

Where to buy accessories

Most car manufacturers have an accessories catalogue, and many contain everything you could ever possibly need!

Obviously, manufacturer's accessories will be designed specifically for your car - for example, tailor-made floor mats should fit perfectly and may incorporate your car's logo – however, this luxury usually comes at a price. You'll find that you can buy good-quality accessories from car accessory shops and motor factors far more cheaply than from an authorised dealer. Accessories sold by a reputable shop are usually of the same standard as the car manufacturer's own products – it's really a matter of personal choice.

Sometimes you can save money by buying second-hand accessories, but you need to be careful. It's a good idea to steer clear of second-hand electrical components, because it's going to be very difficult to tell whether or not they're in good condition, and if they aren't, they're likely to be difficult to repair. Beware of buying accessories from market stalls or car boot sales as there's little chance of getting your money back if they prove to be faulty or incomplete.

Buying the right accessories

If you go to buy any accessory which is likely to be specific to your car (such as roof racks, towing hitches, etc), make sure that you have enough information to hand to ensure that you buy the correct components. You will normally need to provide the make, model, and the date of registration of your car, and you may need to provide the Vehicle Identification Number or Chassis Number – your car's handbook will show you where to look for these, and they can also be found on the registration document.

With some accessories, it's probably worth paying to have them professionally fitted. Accessories such as car phones and alarm systems can be complicated to fit, and the work may involve removing interior trim panels and tapping into the vehicle wiring. If you feel confident that you can tackle these sorts of jobs yourself, make sure that you follow the manufacturer's instructions. If you're having an accessory fitted professionally, and the work involves tampering with any part of the car, make sure that the work will be covered by a warranty.

If you're going to replace any of the car's standard components (such as the steering wheel or roadwheels), make sure you keep the old components (if they're in good condition), then you can refit them when you sell or trade-in the car. You can keep the accessories for your next car, or sell them separately.

Warranties

If your car is relatively new, you need to be careful that you don't invalidate the warranty by fitting non-approved accessories. This is particularly important with accessories such as alarm systems where fitting involves tampering with the car's wiring, or aftermarket sunroofs, where the body panels have to be drilled and cut (this may invalidate the manufacturer's corrosion warranty).

Insurance

If you're fitting expensive accessories (in-car entertainment, or expensive alloy wheels), make sure that you tell your insurance company, otherwise the accessories might not be covered if they're stolen or damaged.

If you're planning to fit trim parts, such as sporty body kits, or spoilers, bear in mind that this could affect your car insurance policy – you'll normally have to pay an increased premium if the car bodywork has been modified, and if you don't declare the modifications to your insurance company, they may not pay up if you have to make a claim!

Getting ready for winter

Winter puts extra strain on a car, and any minor problems which have been hiding are likely to become more obvious and cause trouble once winter gets a grip. In cold conditions, it takes more power to start the engine, and you'll be using the heater and demister more often – this takes its toll on the battery.

Driving in wintry conditions

If you're going to drive in severe cold, or snowy and icy conditions, make sure you're properly equipped. The weather can worsen very quickly in winter, so even if it looks OK when you set off, be prepared!

When driving on slippery roads, drive slowly, smoothly and gently – accelerate gently, steer gently and brake gently.

TELL SOMEONE WHERE YOU'RE GOING, what route you're taking and what time you're expecting to arrive at your destination.

MAKE SURE YOU HAVE A FULL TANK OF FUEL – this will allow you to keep the engine running for warmth (through the heating system), without fear of running out of fuel, if you get delayed or stuck.

CARRY WARM CLOTHES AND BLANKETS to keep you warm if you get stuck. A bar of chocolate could also come in handy.

CARRY DE-ICER FLUID, a scraper, jump leads and a tow rope.

PACK SOME PIECES OF OLD SACKING, or similar material, which you can place under the wheels to give better traction if you get stuck.

PACK A SHOVEL, in case you need to dig yourself out of trouble.

USE SNOW CHAINS OR STUDDED TYRES. In some areas, it's compulsory to use snow chains or studded tyres on certain roads (or even all roads!) – note, however, that it may also be compulsory to remove them again when you reach roads which are unaffected by ice or snow (this applies to many alpine roads at certain times of the year).

What to check before winter starts

CHECK THE COOLANT MIXTURE

If the coolant (antifreeze and water) freezes, it could wreck your engine. A garage can check the coolant for you, or you can buy a simple and inexpensive coolant tester – refer to "Fluids and filters" for details of how to check the coolant mixture. Except in an emergency, never fill your cooling system with plain water, even in summer – antifreeze stops corrosion inside the engine as well as protecting against the cold.

CHECK THE BATTERY

Battery failure is the most common source of trouble in winter. Check that the battery is in good condition, then clean the battery lead connections, and make sure they're tight. If the battery shows signs that it might be getting towards the end of its life, fit a new one before winter starts. Refer to "Batteries" for details of how to check a battery, battery charging, and what to look for when buying a new battery.

CHECK THE WIPERS AND WASHERS

You'll use them a lot more in winter. Make sure the wiper blades are in good condition (new ones aren't expensive, so it's well worth renewing them at the start of every winter anyway). Check the windscreen (and tailgate, if you have one) washer system. Make sure the washer jets aren't blocked, and that they spray onto the screen, not over the top of the roof or onto the bonnet! Refer to "Windows, wipers and mirrors" for details. Always keep the washer fluid topped up – see "Fluids and filters".

CHECK THE COOLING SYSTEM HOSES

Look for signs of damage or leaks, and have any problem hoses renewed. Refer to "Keeping the engine cool" for details of how to check and repair hoses.

CHECK THE DRIVEBELT(S)

Look for damage, and check the tension of the belt(s). Refer to "The engine" for details.

CHECK ALL FLUIDS AND FILTERS

Top up or renew if necessary. Refer to "Fluids and filters " for details.

CHECK ALL THE LIGHTS AND INDICATORS

Make sure that they work properly, and replace any blown bulbs. Refer to "Lights and indicators" for details.

Getting ready for a holiday

If you're taking your car on holiday, you want to be able to relax, so before you set off, it's a good idea to carry out all the checks mentioned in "What to check before winter starts" – this will reduce the possibility of any unexpected breakdowns. Make sure you're carrying all you need to get you out of trouble, particularly if you're travelling abroad – refer to "Things you should always carry" for details.

Don't overload your car. When you're loading, make sure any items you're likely to need during your journey (including your tool kit) are packed so that they're easily accessible.

Travelling abroad

Insurance

Check on the legal requirements for the country you're visiting, and always tell your insurance company that you're taking the car abroad. If you're travelling in the European Community (EC), most insurance policies automatically give only the minimum legally-required cover. If you want the same level of cover as you have at home, you'll usually have to obtain an internationally-recognised certificate of insurance ("Green card"), often for a small charge.

It's a good idea to take out medical insurance. Not all countries have a free emergency medical service, and you could find yourself faced with a large unexpected bill. With a travel insurance policy, you're usually covered for any money lost if you have to cancel your holiday, and your luggage may also be covered against loss or theft. Make sure you take time to read the small print so that you know exactly what's covered!

Recovery and breakdown costs can be far higher abroad. Most of the motoring organisations will be able to provide insurance cover which could save you a lot of inconvenience and expense if you break down.

Driving laws

Make sure you're familiar with the driving laws in the country you're visiting – the penalties for breaking the law may be severe! You may be legally required to carry certain safety equipment such as spare light bulbs, a warning triangle and a first aid kit.

If you're driving on the opposite side of the road from normal, you'll need to fit headlight beam deflectors to avoid dazzling other drivers.

Make sure that you know the appropriate speed limits, and note that in some countries, there's an absolute ban on driving after drinking any alcohol.

Fuel

The type and quality of fuel available varies from country to country. Check on availability, and find out what fuel pump markings to look for to give you the correct type and grade of fuel for your car.

Documents

Always carry your passport, driving licence, vehicle registration document, vehicle test certificate, and insurance certificate(s) (including medical and breakdown insurance, where applicable).

Make sure that all the documents are valid, and that the car tax and vehicle test certificate don't run out whilst you're abroad.

Before travelling, check in case any special documents or permits are required. You may need a visa to visit some countries, and an international driving permit (available from the major motoring organisations) may be required.

Plan ahead

It's a good idea to plan your route before travelling, and have a good road map to hand. Many different maps and guides are available, and most of the motoring organisations will provide a set of directions to your destination, for a small charge, or sometimes free if you're a member. In some countries, you'll have to pay tolls to use certain roads.

If you're travelling a long way, make sure you allow time for any hold-ups, and make sure you take a break if you start to feel tired. If you're on a long journey and you have children in the car, make sure you can keep them amused.

Safety

Road accidents claim thousands of lives every year. The genuine accident which is nobody's fault and could not have been avoided is in fact very rare. Most accidents don't happen, they are caused. Young drivers have more than their share of incidents, due to a combination of inexperience and bravado, which is why their insurance premiums are so high.

Working on your car is nothing like as dangerous as driving it, but it can still be risky if you are unaware of particular hazards. This chapter sets out to encourage a safety-conscious attitude, which can and should be applied to almost every activity you undertake.

Safety when you're driving

These days, car manufacturers are paying more attention to safety. Many cars are fitted with safety devices such as side impact protection bars, seat belt tensioners and airbags, but it's still down to the driver to avoid having an accident in the first place!

You can reduce the risk of being involved in an accident when driving just by being aware of some of the risks which can be avoided.

Before starting a journey

It's important to make sure that you're comfortable, and that you can concentrate on driving without any unnecessary distractions. Make sure that your seat is comfortably positioned, and that the rear view mirrors are adjusted so that you have a clear view behind the car. If the car has an adjustable steering column, adjust it so that the wheel can be reached comfortably, and turned easily without stretching.

Check that you can see clearly through the windscreen and windows – clean the glass if necessary, and in winter, if the car windows are iced up or covered in snow, don't drive the car until they're clear.

Check that there are no distracting reflections in the windscreen or rear window.

If you're tired, or if you've been drinking alcohol recently, or taking medication, are you fit to drive? These can all reduce your co-ordination, increase your reaction time, and affect your judgement. Don't take any chances!

Finally, before you set off, check that all your passengers are comfortable.

During a journey

When you're on a journey it can sometimes be very difficult to maintain concentration, especially on a motorway, when there's no need to change gear or brake, and all you have to do is steer.

CONCENTRATE AND THINK AHEAD
– always be prepared for the unexpected.

DRIVE AT A SAFE SPEED TO SUIT THE ROAD CONDITIONS
– don't break the speed limit.

SLOW DOWN
– in heavy traffic or bad weather conditions.

DON'T DRIVE TOO CLOSE TO THE VEHICLE IN FRONT
– multiple pile-ups on motorways are usually caused by vehicles driving too fast, and following each other too closely.

USE YOUR MIRRORS REGULARLY
– you need to know what's happening behind you as well as in front.

ALWAYS SIGNAL YOUR MANOEUVRES CLEARLY AND IN PLENTY OF TIME
– check your mirrors first, and don't make any sudden moves.

STOP AS SOON AS POSSIBLE IF YOU FEEL TIRED
– wind down a window for fresh air, and turn down the heater. If you feel tired on a motorway, stop at the next service station, or turn off at the next junction – don't stop on the hard shoulder unless it's an emergency.

STAY CALM
– if other drivers annoy you, or seem to be annoyed with you. "Road rage" is now a significant problem. Don't be drawn into a confrontation, and if someone starts following you, head for a busy town centre, or a police station – don't try to drive fast to "shake off" your pursuer, and don't drive to your home. If you have to stop, lock all the car doors and close the windows, and stay inside the car.

IF YOU BREAK DOWN . . . refer to "What to do if you break down".

IF YOU'RE INVOLVED IN AN ACCIDENT . . . refer to "What to do at the scene of an accident".

Seat belts

The risk of serious injury if you have an accident is much higher if you travel without the seat belts fastened.

There are a few things to think about when wearing a seat belt:

● The seat belt webbing mustn't be twisted.
● The upper part of the belt must pass diagonally across the wearer's shoulder and chest.
● The lower part of the belt must fit closely across the wearer's hips, not the abdomen!
● Don't use any clips or fasteners which prevent the belt from touching the wearer's body.
● NEVER travel with a child sitting on a passenger's lap.

Check the seat belts occasionally (for instance, when the car is serviced) as follows:

Check that the webbing is not twisted.

Check that the belts are not cut or fraying, and that they retract freely.

If the webbing is dirty, clean it using soapy water, then allow it to dry in the shade. NEVER use strong detergents, bleach, or chemicals, and make sure that the retractors don't get wet.

After even a moderate impact, have the seat belts replaced. Many cars have seat belt tensioners which pull the belt tight against the wearer if there's an impact. If the tensioner mechanism has been activated, the seat belt must be renewed.

Child seats

Child seats must conform to national safety standards and be fixed in accordance with their maker's instructions – usually by means of existing seat belts (see "Carrying Children").

Airbags

Many modern cars have airbags fitted as standard equipment, a small explosive charge rapidly inflates a bag which cushions the driver and/or passenger against an impact with the steering wheel or facia. A few high specification cars from some manufacturers have additional side airbags,

Most airbags are electronically controlled, with an electronic control unit which measures the car's speed and its deceleration using various sensors. Using the inputs from the sensors, the control unit can decide whether or not the deceleration is due to a frontal impact – this avoids the airbag(s) being activated if the car is hit from behind, or if you kick the bumper!

When an airbag is activated, the sensors trigger an inflator which releases a gas. The gas rapidly inflates the woven nylon airbag, which fully inflates in a fraction of a second. The airbag begins to deflate immediately, to prevent suffocation, and so that the occupants can get out of the car quickly.

Once an airbag has been activated, it will obviously need to be renewed, which can be expensive. DON'T try to renew an airbag yourself – it must be done by an authorised dealer.

Airbags usually have a safe working life of about ten years, and they must be renewed by an authorised dealer at the end of this time.

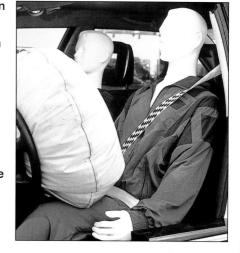

Usually, an airbag warning light will be fitted, either on the instrument panel or on the airbag unit itself – if the warning light comes on, this shows that there's a fault in the control system. In this case, you should take the car to an authorised dealer to have the airbag system checked as soon as possible.

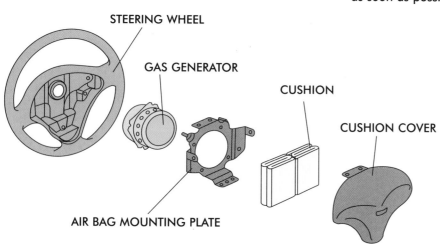

STEERING WHEEL

GAS GENERATOR

CUSHION

CUSHION COVER

AIR BAG MOUNTING PLATE

WARNINGS

- NEVER try to tamper with the airbag.
- DON'T carry out any work close to an airbag which could transmit excessive heat, shocks or jolts to the steering wheel or facia.
- NEVER place a small child or a frail elderly person in the front seat of a car equipped with an airbag.

Safety when you're checking your car

Working on your car can be dangerous, so this page shows just some of the possible risks and hazards, to help you avoid any mishaps or injuries.

Very hot water

Scalding

- Don't remove the coolant filler cap while the engine's hot.
- When draining oil or fluid, remember that it may be hot.

DANGER Hot

Burning

- Beware of burns from the exhaust system and from any part of the engine. Brake components can also be extremely hot after use.
- All types of air conditioning refrigerant can cause skin burns.

DANGER Petroleum mixture giving off a flammable heavy vapour

Fire

- Don't let fuel spill onto a hot engine or manifold. Don't smoke or allow naked lights (including pilot lights) anywhere near a car being worked on. Also beware of creating sparks.
- Fuel vapour is heavier than air, so don't work on the fuel system with the car over an inspection pit.
- The commonest cause of vehicle fires is an electrical overload or short-circuit. Take care when repairing or modifying the vehicle wiring.
- Keep a fire extinguisher of a suitable type handy.

DANGER Electric shock risk

Electric shock

- Don't work on the ignition system with the engine running or the ignition switched on.
- Make sure that any mains-operated equipment is earthed, when applicable. Mains power points should be protected by a circuit breaker.

Crushing

- Don't take risks when working under or near a raised car.
- Take extra care if loosening or tightening nuts or bolts when the car is on stands.
- In an emergency such as roadside wheel changing, slide the spare wheel under the car to provide some support if the jack slips.

DANGER Harmful fumes

Fume or gas intoxication

- Exhaust fumes are poisonous. Never run the engine in a confined space such as a garage with the doors shut.
- Fuel vapour is also poisonous, as are the vapours from some cleaning solvents and paint thinners.

Dangerous substance

Poisonous or irritant substances

- Avoid skin contact with battery acid and with any fuel, fluid or lubricant, especially antifreeze, brake hydraulic fluid and diesel fuel.
- Wear gloves or use a barrier cream if contact with oil is expected.
- Some types of air conditioning refrigerant form a poisonous gas if exposed to a naked flame (including a cigarette).

The battery

- Batteries contain sulphuric acid, which is poisonous and corrosive.
- The hydrogen gas given off by the battery is highly explosive.
- When charging or jump starting, observe any special precautions specified by the battery maker.

Asbestos

Asbestos dust is cancerous if inhaled or swallowed. Asbestos may be found in gaskets and in brake and clutch linings.

Airbags

Airbags can cause injury if they go off accidentally.

Do

- wear eye protection.
- wear gloves or use barrier cream.
- get someone to periodically check that all is well.
- keep clothing, etc, well out of the way of moving parts.
- remove rings, watch, etc, before working on the car.
- ensure that any lifting equipment is adequate.
- mop up fluid spills immediately.

Don't

- try to lift a component which might be too heavy.
- rush to finish a job, or try to take shortcuts.
- use poorly-fitting tools which might slip.
- leave tools or parts lying around.

Troubleshooting

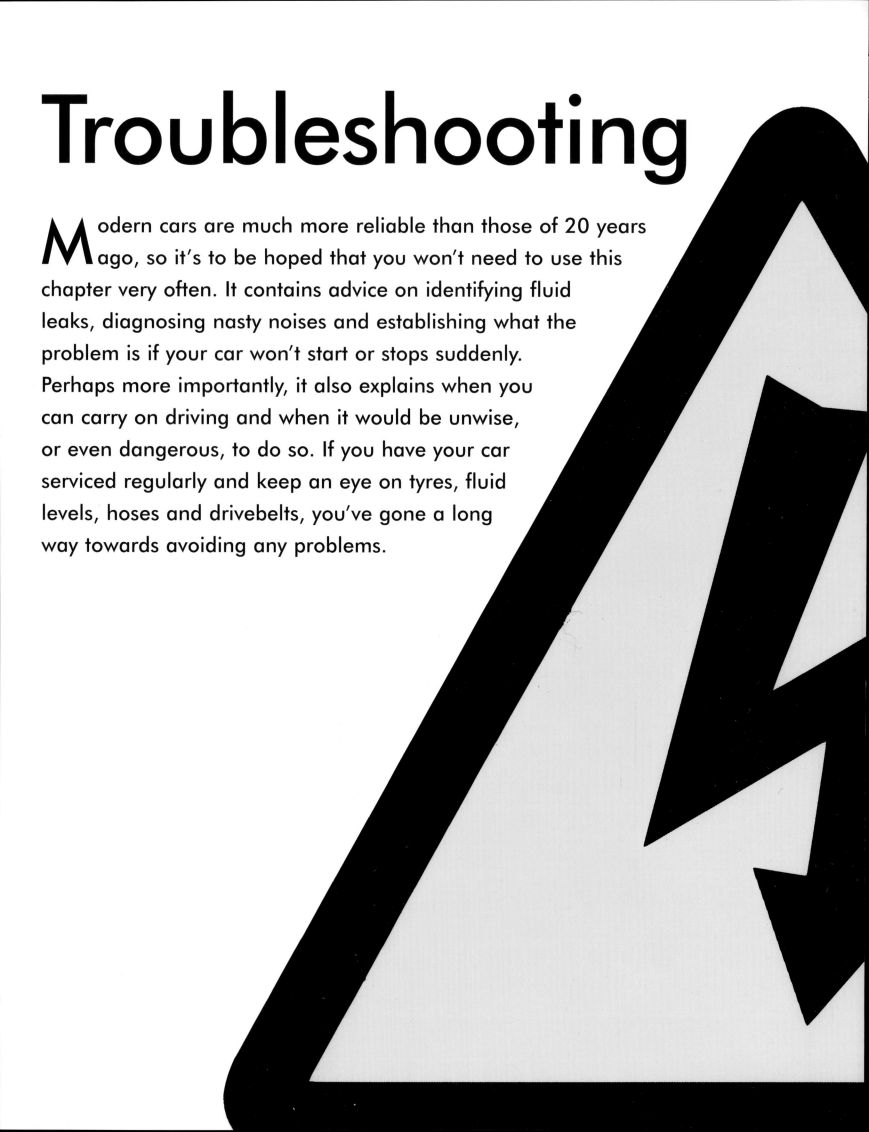

Modern cars are much more reliable than those of 20 years ago, so it's to be hoped that you won't need to use this chapter very often. It contains advice on identifying fluid leaks, diagnosing nasty noises and establishing what the problem is if your car won't start or stops suddenly. Perhaps more importantly, it also explains when you can carry on driving and when it would be unwise, or even dangerous, to do so. If you have your car serviced regularly and keep an eye on tyres, fluid levels, hoses and drivebelts, you've gone a long way towards avoiding any problems.

Leaks

A leak may show up as a stain under your car, or you may be forever topping-up one of the fluids (see "Fluids and filters"). So how do you tell if a leak is serious, or something you can live with for a while?

Apart from an obvious pool of liquid under your car, if you have to top up any of the fluids regularly, this may also indicate a leak. If you have to top up the engine oil regularly, the engine could be burning oil – see "All about oil".

DIESEL FUEL

Symptoms

Diesel fuel has a distinctive oily smell (like domestic heating oil), and is a clear, oily substance. As with petrol, a recently filled tank may leak a little due to expansion. Any other leak is cause for concern.

Is it OK to drive the car?

DON'T drive the car until the leak's been fixed.

Is it easy to fix?

If the leak's coming from a fuel line connection, you might be able to cure it by tightening the connection (or hose clip) if not, don't try to fix the leak yourself, call for help.

BRAKE FLUID

Symptoms

Brake fluid is clear, thin and almost watery. Old brake fluid gradually darkens. Compare the leak with the contents of the brake fluid reservoir. Leaks usually come from around the wheels, the brake line connections under the car, or the brake master cylinder in the engine compartment.

Is it OK to drive the car?

DON'T drive the car if you think there might be a brake fluid leak.

Is it easy to fix?

Dismantling will be required to fix this, call for help.

CLUTCH FLUID

Symptoms

Leaks usually come from hydraulic line connections, or from failed seals in the hydraulic components.

Is it OK to drive the car?

It's OK to drive with a minor leak, but if you lose all the fluid, the clutch won't work.

Is it easy to fix?

You might be able to fix a leaky fluid line union by tightening it. The leak could be due to a failed fluid seal in one of the clutch hydraulic components. Dismantling will be required to fix this – call for help.

PETROL

Symptoms

Petrol has a strong and distinctive smell, so a leak should be obvious. If you've just filled up with petrol on a hot day, and the car's standing in the sun, the petrol may expand, and leak out through the fuel tank breather. Petrol can also leak if you park a car with a full tank on a steep slope.

If the leak's not due to either of the above causes, have it investigated straight away.

Is it OK to drive the car?

DON'T drive the car until the leak's been fixed.

Is it easy to fix?

If the leak's coming from a hose connection, you might be able to cure it by tightening the connection (or hose clip) – if not, don't try to fix the leak yourself, call for help.

How to identify a leak (continued)

ENGINE OIL

Symptoms

Engine oil is usually black, unless it's recently been changed. Clean oil is usually clear or green. Compare the leak with the oil on the end of the oil level dipstick. The most common sources of leaks are the oil drain plug, the oil filter, and the sump gasket under the engine.

Is it OK to drive the car?

You can drive with a minor oil leak, but keep an eye on the oil level.

Is it easy to fix?

If the leak's coming from the oil drain plug or the filter, try tightening the plug or filter (as applicable). If the leak's coming from anywhere else, have it checked as soon as possible.

WATER

If a leak looks like clear water, and your car has air conditioning, it may not be a leak, but condensation from the air conditioning. A lot of condensation can be produced on a hot day, which may look like a major leak.

Also see "Coolant" and "Washer fluid".

AUTOMATIC TRANSMISSION FLUID

Symptoms

The fluid may be clear or a reddish-brown colour. Compare the leak with the fluid on the end of the transmission fluid level dipstick. Leaks usually come from the transmission casing, or from fluid lines running to the fluid cooler (this could be mounted on the transmission, or incorporated in the radiator).

Is it OK to drive the car?

You can drive with a minor leak, but keep an eye on the fluid level.

Is it easy to fix?

You might be able to fix a leaky connection by tightening it. Any other leaks should be checked out by a garage.

MANUAL TRANSMISSION OR FINAL DRIVE OIL

Symptoms

The oil is usually a tan colour or reddish-pink, although old oil may darken. Transmission oil is thicker than engine oil, and often has a very sickly smell, especially when hot.

Is it OK to drive the car?

You can drive with a minor leak, but if the oil level gets too low, it can cause serious transmission damage.

Is it easy to fix?

Most leaks are due to failed gaskets or oil seals, so dismantling is usually required to fix the leak – get a garage to have a look as soon as you can.

WASHER FLUID

Symptoms

Washer fluid usually contains a coloured dye, and has a strong smell of detergent, alcohol or ammonia. The leak could be due to a poor pipe connection, or a leaky washer pump seal in the fluid reservoir.

Is it OK to drive the car?

Yes!

Is it easy to fix?

Yes, but it might be tricky to get to the fluid pipes and reservoir.

SHOCK ABSORBER FLUID

Symptoms

Usually shows up as a dark stain on the shock absorber body.

Is it OK to drive the car?

Yes, but you may have a poor ride, and poor handling – take care!

Is it easy to fix?

You'll need two new shock absorbers – ie, if one rear shock absorber is leaking, you should renew both rear shock absorbers. Consult a garage or a fast-fit specialist.

POWER STEERING FLUID

Symptoms

The fluid is usually clear or reddish-brown. Compare the leak with the contents of the power steering fluid reservoir. Leaks usually come from fluid line connections, the power steering pump, or the steering gear.

Is it OK to drive the car?

You can drive with a minor leak, but keep an eye on the fluid level.

Is it easy to fix?

To fix a leaky fluid line connection, try tightening it. If the pump or steering gear is leaking, you'll need advice from a garage.

COOLANT

Symptoms

Coolant usually contains a bright-coloured dye, and has a strong, sickly sweet smell. Old coolant may be rusty or dirty brown, and there may be a white crystalline deposit around the leak. Leaks usually come from a hose, the radiator, or the heater inside the car (you'll smell coolant when you switch the heater on).

Is it OK to drive the car?

You can drive with a minor leak, but if you lose too much coolant, the engine could overheat.

Is it easy to fix?

Sometimes you can stop a leak by tightening up a hose clip. If a hose is split, you might be able to make an emergency repair using a repair bandage. If the radiator or heater is leaking, you may be able to fix it temporarily by using a radiator sealant.

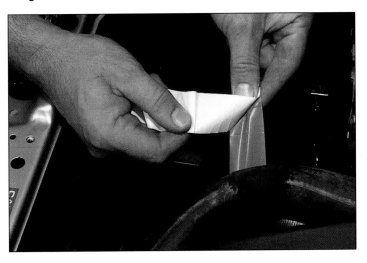

GREASE

Symptoms

Grease is usually black or grey, thick and very sticky! You may find it under the car if it's leaked from the driveshaft rubber gaiters or steering gear gaiters.

Is it OK to drive the car?

Yes, but if much grease has been lost, the driveshaft or steering gear could be damaged through lack of lubrication.

Is it easy to fix?

Some dismantling will be required, so consult a garage.

What's that noise?

A strange noise could spell trouble, or it could just be an annoying distraction – so how do you tell? Here's a guide to help you to identify noises and decide what to do about them, even if you just want to describe the problem to a mechanic.

NOISE	POSSIBLE CAUSE	REMARKS
Noises from the exhaust		
Light "puffing" or blowing noise when accelerating or decelerating, or when engine is idling	Small hole or crack in exhaust system	Repair temporarily with exhaust putty. Go to exhaust specialist for advice.
Sudden increase in noise, especially when accelerating and decelerating	Hole or crack in exhaust system, or failed silencer	Repair temporarily with exhaust bandage. Go to exhaust specialist for advice.
Metallic rattling or thumping over bumps, or when accelerating and decelerating	Loose or broken exhaust mounting	Repair temporarily with wire. Go to exhaust specialist for advice.
Noises from the brakes		
Light squeaking when applying brakes gently for the first time of the day	Normal characteristic of disc brakes	Could be normal.
Squealing whenever brakes are applied	Could be first sign of excessively worn brake friction material	Ask your garage to check – possibly cured by applying special brake grease to the metal brake component surfaces. Renew brake pads or shoes if required.
Deep metallic scraping when brakes are applied, or when the brakes aren't in use	Excessively worn brake components Trapped stone or dirt between brake disc and pad	Have your garage investigate without delay before furtherdamage occurs.
Chattering or tapping when brakes are applied	Contaminated brake friction material	Damaged brake discs or drums. Have your garage investigate without delay.
Noises from the suspension		
Clunks or rattles when driving over bumps	Worn or damaged suspension or steering components Loose or broken exhaust mounting	Probably not urgent, but have your garage investigate before too long.
Rumbling, growling or clicking noises when turning corners	Worn wheel bearing(s) Worn driveshaft joint (front-wheel-drive cars)	Probably not urgent, but may cause further damage if neglected.
"Hissing" noise when driving slowly over bumps	Badly worn shock absorbers	Drive carefully until new shock absorbers have been fitted - handling and ride may be poor.
Constant clicking noise	Stone embedded in tyre Wheel fouling brake or suspension component	Take the stone out with your penknife! If it's not a stone, seek advice.

NOISE	POSSIBLE CAUSE	REMARKS
Noises from the engine compartment		
Squealing	Loose or worn auxiliary drivebelt or timing belt	Probably not urgent, but get it fixed before it breaks.
Continuous hum or whine	Auxiliary drivebelt or timing belt too tight Alternator, coolant pump or power steering pump worn	Probably not urgent, but get it fixed before it gets worse.
Rhythmic slapping when the engine is cold	"Piston slap"	Not a problem as long as it stops when the engine warms up.
Light tapping from the top of the engine	Valve clearances incorrect (too large)	Not urgent, but have them adjusted at the next service.
Rhythmic metallic thumping or thudding	Worn engine bearings or camshaft	May be a serious problem. Have it investigated without delay.
High-pitched metallic rattle when engine is under load (accelerating or driving uphill)	Engine "pinking" or "pre-ignition" (poor quality fuel or wrong fuel type, or ignition system fault)	Drive gently until you can fill up with good fuel or have the ignition system checked.
Noises from the transmission		
Whine or howl from manual transmission in neutral, quietens or disappears when clutch pedal is depressed	Worn transmission bearing	You can still drive, but have it fixed before it gets much worse.
Whine or howl from manual transmission when clutch pedal is depressed, quietens or disappears when pedal is released	Worn clutch release bearing	You can still drive, but have it fixed before it gets much worse.
Squealing from manual transmission as clutch is engaged or released	Incorrectly adjusted clutch Worn clutch	If adjustment doesn't cure the problem, have it fixed before it gets worse.
Whine or howl from automatic transmission in neutral	Low transmission fluid level Worn or damaged transmission	Check the fluid level. If that's OK, have the transmission checked without delay.
Howl or whine when accelerating or decelerating	Low transmission oil/fluid level Worn bearing in transmission Worn or damaged differential	Check the oil level. If that's OK, you can probably carry on driving for a while, but have the transmission checked before something breaks.
"Graunching" sound from manual transmission when changing gear	Incorrectly adjusted clutch Worn synchromesh units in transmission Badly worn gears	If clutch adjustment doesn't cure it, you probably need a new transmission.

Why did it stop?

Although there isn't space here to give a comprehensive fault-finding guide, if the engine stops, it's useful to have some idea of where to start looking for the problem.

If the engine stops running suddenly as if the ignition has been switched off, it's probably due to an ignition system fault, whereas if the engine splutters or misfires before finally stopping, it's usually a fuel system fault. The following chart will give you a few clues.

SYMPTOM	POSSIBLE CAUSE
Engine suddenly stops as if switched off	Faulty ignition switch (or switch accidentally turned off!) Loose or broken connection or wire in ignition system Faulty ignition system component(s) Loose or broken battery earth connection
Engine splutters or misfires, loses power and stops	Fuel tank empty! Fuel cut-off switch activated (see "What to do if your car won't start") Dirt or water in fuel lines Faulty fuel system component(s) Water on ignition system components (in bad weather or after going through a flood) Faulty ignition system component(s)
Engine makes unpleasant noises and stops	Mechanical failure (such as broken timing belt)

Why won't it start?

If the engine won't start, work through the following flow chart to try to find a clue to the cause – you may not be able to fix the problem yourself, but at least you'll be able to give a mechanic a few clues about the cause of the problem.

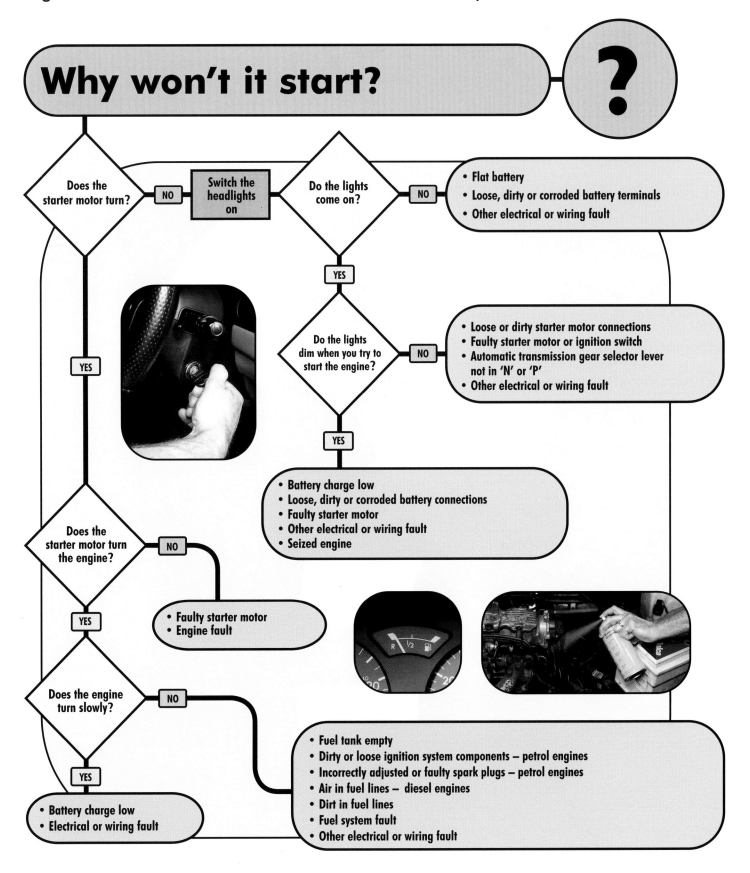

Why won't it start? ?

Does the starter motor turn? **NO** → Switch the headlights on → Do the lights come on? **NO** →
- Flat battery
- Loose, dirty or corroded battery terminals
- Other electrical or wiring fault

YES ↓

Do the lights dim when you try to start the engine? **NO** →
- Loose or dirty starter motor connections
- Faulty starter motor or ignition switch
- Automatic transmission gear selector lever not in 'N' or 'P'
- Other electrical or wiring fault

YES ↓
- Battery charge low
- Loose, dirty or corroded battery connections
- Faulty starter motor
- Other electrical or wiring fault
- Seized engine

Does the starter motor turn the engine? **NO** →
- Faulty starter motor
- Engine fault

YES ↓

Does the engine turn slowly? **NO** →
- Fuel tank empty
- Dirty or loose ignition system components – petrol engines
- Incorrectly adjusted or faulty spark plugs – petrol engines
- Air in fuel lines – diesel engines
- Dirt in fuel lines
- Fuel system fault
- Other electrical or wiring fault

YES ↓
- Battery charge low
- Electrical or wiring fault

In an emergency

Nobody sets off in their car intending to break down or have an accident. Punctures are much rarer than they used to be, laminated windscreens don't shatter and even running out of fuel is easier to avoid now that most cars have low fuel level warning lights. Car crime, on the other hand, is a persistent problem almost everywhere.

The following pages contain some useful advice on what to do in various emergency situations. Most of it is common sense, but it's probably worth reading through it at leisure to make sure that you would know what to do in any of the situations mentioned.

What to do if you break down

If you're unfortunate enough to break down on the road, try to keep calm, and think logically. You may not know what's wrong, but don't panic – the majority of breakdowns are caused by simple problems, which can easily be fixed at the roadside by a good mechanic.

The following advice has been written with women driving alone particularly in mind, but much of it applies to any driver.

On ordinary roads

Try to stop where there are other people about. If possible, move the car out of the way of other traffic, then switch on the hazard warning lights, and set up your warning triangle if you have one. Lift up the bonnet – this will indicate to other motorists and any passing police patrol vehicles that you have a problem.

NEVER hitch a lift.

If you need to walk to a phone, take any children with you. Give details of:

1. Your location
2. Your car make, colour and registration number
3. The likely cause of the breakdown, or any symptoms
4. Whether you're alone, or with young children
5. Your motoring organisation membership number (if applicable)

Don't worry if you don't have all this information.

Return to your car and, unless there's a danger of other traffic hitting it, stay inside, lock the doors, close the windows, and wait for help.

If someone stops to offer help, talk to them through a closed window until you're absolutely sure that you can trust them. ALWAYS ask for identification. It must be a personal decision to accept help – or not.

On a motorway

Pull onto the hard shoulder and park well away from the main carriageway. Switch on the hazard warning lights. If you don't have a mobile phone, get out of the car using the passenger's side door (taking any children with you) and walk to the nearest emergency telephone, keeping well in to the side of the hard shoulder. Arrows on marker posts at the edge of the hard shoulder indicate the direction to the nearest emergency phone – the phones will link you to a control centre. When you use the phone, face oncoming traffic.

If you do have a mobile phone, get out of the car using the passenger's side door (again, take any children with you), then use your phone to contact your motoring organisation or the police.

Tell the operator on the other end of the phone:

1. Your exact location (the emergency phones on a motorway are numbered)
2. Your car make, colour and registration number
3. The likely cause of the breakdown, or any symptoms
4. Whether you're alone, or with young children
5. Your motoring organisation membership number (if applicable)

Don't worry if you don't have all this information.

Return to your car, but stand well away, and don't get in unless you feel at risk – fatal accidents occur on the hard shoulder.

Breakdown assistance

Although it may seem expensive at first glance, joining one of the breakdown assistance organisations is very worthwhile, and could save you a lot of hassle and money. If you break down, and you don't belong to one of the motoring organisations, you'll have to arrange for roadside assistance, or recovery to a garage – this will almost certainly cost you more than a year's membership fee! Even if you only choose the basic minimum membership package from one of the leading motoring organisations, you'll easily save more than your membership fee the first time you have to call on their services. Some organisations will give you the option of being transported to your intended destination, or back home and, for an additional fee, will also provide breakdown cover if you take your car abroad. There's also the "peace-of-mind" factor when you know that help is never far away.

How to change a wheel

Changing a wheel is straightforward provided you know where the tools and spare wheel are kept, and how to use the jack. If you've just bought the car, or if you've never changed a wheel before, it's worth practising at home, then you'll know exactly what to do if you get a flat tyre.

1 Apply the handbrake, engage first gear (set automatic transmission to "P"), then chock the wheel diagonally opposite the one to be changed.

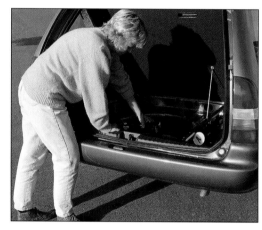

2 Get out the spare wheel, vehicle jack and wheelbrace. They are generally located in the luggage area, under a cover in the floor (check your car's handbook for details).

3 Where applicable, remove the wheel trim/cover. Use the wheelbrace to loosen each wheel bolt/nut on the affected wheel by about half a turn.

If you get a flat tyre when you're on a journey, first make sure that the car is parked safely away from traffic. If you're at the side of a busy road, and you can't move the car, it's safer to call for assistance rather than risk an accident. Stop the car, switch on the hazard warning lights, and set up your warning triangle if you have one.

Sometimes it's difficult to loosen the wheel bolts or nuts. You can buy a wheel brace with an extending handle to make things easier, or alternatively, you can carry a length of metal tube to fit over the wheel brace for more leverage.

4 Engage the jack head in the jacking point nearest the affected wheel (check your car's handbook for details). Slide the spare wheel part way under the car, near the wheel to be removed, but out of the way of the jack (this is a safety measure). Raise the jack until the wheel is an inch or two off the ground.

5 Remove the wheel bolts/nuts, and lift off the wheel. Drag out the spare wheel and slide the removed wheel under the car in its place.

8 When you've finished, stow the removed wheel and the tools back in their correct locations. Check the pressure in the "new" tyre, with your gauge or at the next available garage. It's important to get the flat tyre repaired or renewed as soon as possible – don't put it off!

REFITTING A WHEEL

Positioning a wheel can be tricky as you have to support its weight at the same time. If you find this difficult, try resting the wheel on your foot and using it to help you manoeuvre the wheel into postition.

6 Fit the spare wheel, then refit the bolts/nuts, and tighten them until they're just holding the wheel firmly. Remove the wheel from under the car, then lower the jack, and remove it from under the car.

7 Tighten one wheel bolt/nut securely, using the wheelbrace, then tighten the one diagonally opposite. Tighten the other two bolts/nuts in the same way, then refit the wheel trim, where applicable.

Space-saver spare tyres

These tyres are narrower than normal tyres, and are often inflated to a different pressure. There are usually speed and mileage restrictions marked on the tyre, or printed in the car handbook – make sure you observe these restrictions.
If you fit a "space-saver" tyre, have the flat tyre repaired and refitted as soon as possible.

What to do at the scene of an accident

The first priority must be safety. This might seem obvious, but it's easy to overlook certain points which could make the situation worse – always try to think clearly, and don't panic!

1. Further collisions and fire are the main dangers in a road accident

● If possible, warn other traffic.
● Switch on the car's hazard warning flashers.
● Set up a warning triangle a reasonable distance away from the accident to warn approaching drivers. Decide from which direction the approaching traffic will have least warning, and position the triangle accordingly.
● Send someone to warn approaching traffic of the danger, and signal the traffic to slow down.
● Switch off the ignition and make sure no-one smokes. This will reduce the possibility of a fire if there is a petrol leak.

2. Administer first aid if you've been properly trained.

3. Send someone to call the emergency services, and make sure that all the necessary information is given to the operator. Give the exact location of the accident, the number of vehicles and, if applicable, the number of casualties involved.

● Call an ambulance if anyone is seriously injured or trapped.
● Call the fire brigade if you think there is a risk of fire.
● Call the police if any of the above conditions apply. In most cases, the accident must be reported to the police within 24 hours.

4. If you're involved in the accident, provide your personal and vehicle details to anyone having reasonable grounds to ask for them.

Essential details to record

The following details will help you fill in an accident report form for your insurance company, and will help if the police become involved. Inform your insurance company if you're involved in an accident, even if you're not going to make a claim.

1. The name and address of the other driver, and those of the vehicle owner, if different.
2. The name(s) and address(es) of any witness(es). Independent witnesses are especially important.
3. A description of any injury to yourself or anyone else
4. Details of any damage.
5. The other driver's insurance company details.
6. The registration number of the other vehicle.
7. The number of any police officer attending the scene.
8. The location, time and date of the accident.
9. The speed of the vehicles involved.
10. The width of the road, details of road signs, the state of the road, and the weather.
11. Any relevant marks or debris on the road.
12. A rough sketch of the accident.
13. Whether the vehicle occupants were wearing seat belts.
14. If it happened at night or in bad weather, whether vehicle lights or street lights were on.
15. If you have a camera, take pictures.
16. If the other driver refuses to give you their name and address, or if you think that they have committed a criminal offence, inform the police immediately.

What the law says you must do if you have an accident

If you're involved in an accident - which causes damage or injury to any other person, another vehicle, an animal, or roadside property.

1. Stop.
2. Give your own and the vehicle owner's name and address, the registration number of the vehicle, and your insurance details to anyone having reasonable grounds for requiring them.
3. If you don't give your name and address to any such person at the time, report the accident to the police as soon as possible, and in any case within 24 hours.

What to do if your car has been stolen

If you left the car in a car park, are you sure that you've returned to where you left it? This might sound obvious, but large car parks, especially multi-storeys, can be pretty confusing!

The first thing to do if your car has been stolen is to contact the police, giving them the following information:

◆ Your name and address
◆ The make, colour and registration number of your car
◆ The location of your car
◆ The time that you left your car, and the time that you returned
◆ Details of any important or valuable items left in the car

After informing the police, contact your insurance company, and give them the details that you provided to the police – you'll have to fill in a claim form later, but you should inform your insurance company by phone as soon as possible after the incident. Most insurance companies provide a "help-line" - they will often arrange for you to be transported home, as will most of the motoring assistance organisations, if you're a member.

What to do if your car has been broken into

Check to see if anything has been stolen, and write down the details of any stolen items. Next, check your car for damage – is there any damage which will stop you from driving the car (wiring, ignition switch, steering, etc), which may not be obvious at first?

Once you've checked your car, contact the police, and give them the following information:

● Your name and address
● The make, colour and registration number of your car
● The location of your car
● The time that you left your car, and the time that you returned
● Details of any damage, and details of any items stolen

After informing the police, contact your insurance company, and give them the details that you provided to the police – you'll have to fill in a claim form later, but you should inform your insurance company by phone as soon as possible after the incident. Most insurance companies provide a "help-line" – if your car can't be driven, they will often arrange for recovery of your car, as will most of the motoring organisations, if you're a member.

What to do if your car won't start

There aren't many things more frustrating than an engine that won't start - but try to think logically. If you're at home, it's better than being stranded miles from anywhere. If you're a member of one of the motoring organisations, and your membership includes "home-start", now's the time to pick up the phone. If not, run through the following checks.

1 Immobiliser - check that you know how this works, and make sure that you know the starting procedure, otherwise it may seem like you have a "dead" engine.

2 Automatic transmission – the engine won't start unless the selector lever is in the "N" or "P" position. This is a safety feature, and is not a fault.

3 If there's no familiar starter motor sound (or just a clicking noise), then the starter motor may be faulty, or the battery may be flat (see "Batteries").

4 You could be out of fuel (faulty gauges have been known, so don't rely totally on the reading). Consider whether this is a possibility (not if you've just filled up!). See "What to do if you run out of fuel".

5 On some petrol engine cars, there's a cut-off switch which stops the fuel flow in the event of an accident. Sometimes, the switch can be triggered by a pot hole or minor bump – you'll have to reset it manually. Check your car's handbook for details, and try resetting it. Most switches can be reset by pushing a button on the top of the switch.

6 Check for damp ignition leads (try a water-dispersant spray), or worn spark plugs on petrol engines. Other possibilities are air or water in the fuel system (diesel engines), a blocked fuel system, a badly worn engine, or a serious fault – professional help is probably needed at this stage.

What to do if you run out of fuel

Don't keep on trying to start the engine, hoping to pick up the last drops of fuel from the tank – you'll suck air, and possibly dirt from the empty tank into the fuel system, which will make starting even harder when you've filled up!

If you have a can of fuel, switch off the ignition (NO SMOKING!) and empty it into the tank. Operate the starter for about 10 seconds several times, and if the engine now starts, fill the tank at a filling station. If the engine still won't start, dirt or air drawn into the fuel system could be causing problems, in which case you'll probably need professional help.

If you're out in the middle of nowhere, or on a motorway, all's not lost! On a motorway, you can use the emergency telephones to call for help, and if you're a member of one of the motoring organisations, they'll deliver an emergency can of fuel to you.

So why did you run out of fuel? If the fuel gauge indicated plenty of fuel in the tank, have the gauge checked, it's probably faulty. If there's a fuel leak, you should be able to smell the petrol vapour – DON'T drive the car until you've had the problem fixed!

What to do if there's a leak

Refer to "Troubleshooting".

Diesel engine cars

The engine may be difficult to start even when you've refilled the tank. This is due to air being drawn into the fuel lines when the fuel ran out. Most cars are fitted with a hand priming pump (refer to your car's handbook) in the fuel system to get the engine started. Normally, the pump takes the form of a large pushbutton on top of the fuel filter, or a rubber bulb in one of the fuel lines. Switch on the ignition, then pump the priming button or bulb until you feel resistance (this could take more than thirty presses), indicating that the air has been expelled. Try to start the engine with the accelerator fully depressed – the engine should eventually start. If the engine still won't start, air has probably been drawn into the fuel injection pump – fuel lines must be disconnected, so professional help is needed.

What to do if your windscreen breaks

Most cars have "laminated" windscreens. If a laminated windscreen is hit, it may chip or crack, but it should still be possible to see through it clearly, and the glass shouldn't shatter. On older cars without laminated windscreens, the glass is more likely to break or shatter.

Small chips and cracks can often be repaired. If a crack develops, have it repaired as soon as possible (a large crack will mean a new windscreen).

If you can't see clearly, or if the glass shatters, stop in a safe place, and switch on your hazard warning lights. Never try to knock the glass out – you may cut yourself. Don't drive with no windscreen – it will be extremely windy, and you risk being hit by loose glass particles, insects, and road debris.

There are several emergency mobile windscreen repair companies, who will come to your assistance at the roadside if necessary – it's worth keeping the phone number of one of these companies with you. In any case, your insurance company will usually pay for windscreen repair if you pay a small excess.

What to do if the engine overheats

Cars most often overheat when stuck in traffic – keep an eye on the temperature gauge. Overheating can cause serious and expensive engine damage, so watch for the warning signs!

If the temperature gauge is working, the first sign will be the gauge needle creeping towards the red. Sometimes a temperature warning light is fitted. If you notice either of these signs, move the heater control to maximum straight away, and switch the heater blower motor to maximum – this will get rid of some of the heat from the engine. If the temperature doesn't drop, or keeps going up, pull over in a safe place and stop the engine.

In extreme cases, the first sign of overheating may be steam coming from under the bonnet. Pull over and stop as soon as possible. Don't open the bonnet until the steam stops.

If no steam is coming from under the bonnet, open the bonnet to help the heat escape, and wait for the engine to cool down!

A very hot engine takes time to cool, and you'll have to wait at least half-an-hour before the temperature drops to normal.

Check under the car for coolant leakage – coolant is usually brightly coloured (often green, yellow or pink), and will probably be steaming if it's hot!

If there's a leak, call for assistance (see "What to do if you break down").

When the engine has cooled, check the coolant level (see "Fluids and filters") – if there's been no leakage, and no steam, the level will probably be above the "maximum" mark (hot coolant expands). If the coolant level is OK, and there's no leakage, it's safe to carry on driving, but keep an eye on the temperature gauge!

If the level is low, it's time to top up (see "Fluids and filters"). You can use plain water in an emergency. If almost all the coolant has been lost, don't fill the system with cold water whilst the engine is hot, as this might cause engine damage.

What causes overheating?

Apart from simply getting too hot on a summer's day in traffic, here are the most common causes of engine overheating (see "Cooling and heating" for details of how the cooling system works):

◆ Low coolant level
◆ Faulty cooling fan
◆ Leakage
◆ Faulty coolant pump
◆ Broken coolant pump drivebelt (where applicable)

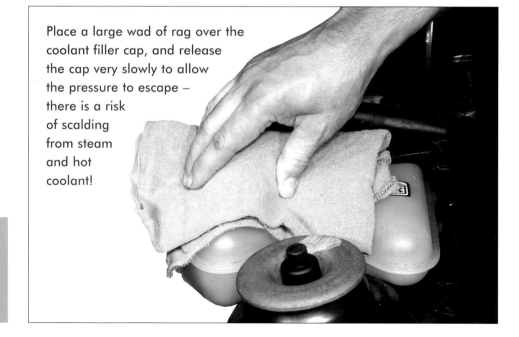

Place a large wad of rag over the coolant filler cap, and release the cap very slowly to allow the pressure to escape – there is a risk of scalding from steam and hot coolant!

What to do if there's a leak

Refer to "Troubleshooting".

Problems with the exhaust

The exhaust doesn't last forever, and you'll have to have part of the system renewed if you keep the car for a few years. There are a number of exhaust specialists who carry out work, with a guarantee, at far cheaper rates than a dealer.

Exhaust hangs down or falls off

If the exhaust rattles or hits the road, it's usually due to a broken mounting. You can carry out a temporary repair using a piece of stout wire.

If the exhaust has broken, you may still be able to support the broken section with wire.

If the exhaust has sheared off completely, you're going to have a noisy drive to the nearest exhaust repair centre!

> **WARNING**
>
> Take care not to burn yourself on a hot exhaust!

Exhaust blowing?

A "blowing" exhaust can usually be heard when accelerating or decelerating. It's annoying, and also means hot gases are escaping from the exhaust – this can damage surrounding components, and is dangerous if the fumes get inside the car (exhaust gases are poisonous!).

The exhaust may blow due to a leaking joint, or because there's a hole in the system.

Temporary repairs can be done using exhaust repair putty, or a repair bandage (follow the instructions supplied), but if there's a hole, the best answer is to have a new exhaust section fitted.

How to tow a car

Special towing eyes are normally provided at the front and rear of the car. Sometimes the towing eyes may be hidden under covers, and some cars have screw-in towing eyes provided in the tool kit – check your car's handbook for details.

Obviously you'll need a suitable tow-rope. It's worth carrying one just in case you ever need it.

If you've never towed before, take note of the following points.

• When being towed - the ignition key must be turned to the "on" position so that the steering lock is released. This will also allow the indicators, horn and brake lights to work. If the battery is flat or there's some other electrical problem, you'll have to use hand signals.

• If you're driving a car that's being towed – the brake servo won't work (because the engine isn't running). This means that you'll have to press the brake pedal harder than usual, so allow for longer braking distances. Also, power steering (where applicable) won't work when the engine isn't running, so you'll need more effort to turn the steering wheel. If the breakdown doesn't stop the engine running, you could allow it to idle so that the brake servo and power steering

> **WARNING**
>
> Don't tow an accident-damaged vehicle - it may be in a dangerous condition.

work normally. On Citroën models with hydraulic suspension (BX, CX, XM, etc), if the engine is not running the brakes won't work.

• If the car being towed has automatic transmission - the gear lever should be moved to the "N" position. Often, the manufacturer recommends that you don't exceed a certain speed or distance - check your car's handbook for details. Ideally, a car with automatic transmission should be towed with the driven wheels off the ground.

• An "On tow" notice should be displayed at the rear of the car on tow.

• Make sure that both drivers know details of the route to be taken before moving off.

• Before moving away - the tow car should be driven slowly forwards to take up any slack in the tow rope.

• The driver of the car on tow should try to keep the tow rope tight at all times – by gently using the brakes if necessary.

• Drive smoothly at all times - especially when moving away from a standstill.

• Allow plenty of time to slow down and stop - especially when approaching junctions and traffic queues.

Tools

A selection of basic tools is essential if you're thinking of maintaining your own car. The tool kit supplied with most cars won't allow you to do much more than change a wheel! Even if you're not going to carry out any maintenance, it's a good idea to carry a few extra tools just in case – if you can't fix a problem yourself, someone else might be able to help if you can supply a screwdriver.

You don't need to buy the most expensive tools, but generally you get what you pay for, and a good quality set of tools will last for many years.

What do I need?

The tools in "Things you should always carry" are what you'll need if you're not planning to do any DIY maintenance.

If you are going to carry out your own basic maintenance, there are a few extra tools you'll need.

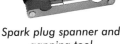

Screwdrivers (flat-blade and crosshead)

Pliers

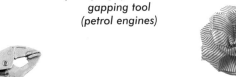

Spanners, or basic socket set (covering range 10 to 19 mm)

Spark plug spanner and gapping tool (petrol engines)

Torch

Self-locking grips

A wad of clean cloth

A toolbox to keep everything together!

12 volt light

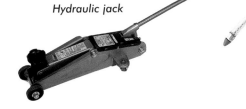
Hydraulic jack

Oil can

Extra tools you'll need will probably include the following:

- A comprehensive socket set (8 to 26 mm)
- Oil filter removal tool
- Sump drain plug tool
- Oil can
- Funnel
- Oil draining container
- Self-locking grips
- Scriber
- Light, with extension lead
- Hydraulic jack
- Axle stands
- Brake bleed nipple spanner
- Brake bleeding kit

- Soft-faced mallet
- Ball pein hammer
- Torque wrench
- Tyre pump
- Small wire brush
- Junior hacksaw
- Fine emery cloth
- Electric drill – with a good range of twist drills
- Overalls
- Old newspapers and clean rags for cleaning and mopping up

Once you've built up a reasonable tool kit, you need to keep the tools in good condition. Never leave tools lying around after they've been used. Take care when using tools, and don't try to use them for a job they're not designed for.

Generally there are safety standards for tools. Usually the packaging, or the tools themselves, will show that they meet a particular standard. You can buy plenty of tools which don't meet any standards, but they're more likely to let you down, and they're unlikely to last as long.

You don't have to buy the most expensive tools, but it's a good idea to steer clear of the very cheap ones.

You'll have to make sensible compromises when choosing tools. If you're on a limited budget, it's best to spend a little more on the tools you're likely to use most often – for instance a good set of spanners should last you a lifetime, whereas a poor quality set will tend to wear, and won't fit properly. Combination spanners (ring one end, open-ended the other) are the best buy if you can afford them, as they give the advantages of both types of spanner.

If you find that you need a special tool which it isn't economic to buy, you may be able to borrow or hire it from a local garage or a tool hire specialist for a reasonable charge.

All about oil

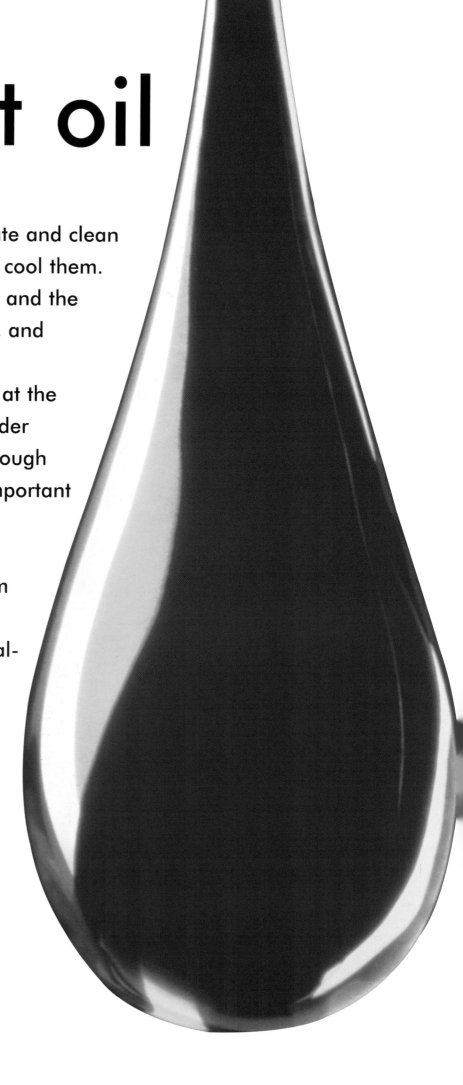

Oil is used in the engine to lubricate and clean the moving parts, and to help to cool them. The oil also helps to prevent corrosion and the build-up of deposits inside the engine, and improves fuel economy.

A pump picks up oil from the sump at the bottom of the engine, and forces it under pressure through the oil filter, then through small passages in the engine to the important parts, and finally back to the sump.

Without oil, the engine would very quickly seize up. The oil provides a film between the engine bearing surfaces - without it, friction from metal-to-metal contact would soon overheat and destroy the bearings, wrecking the engine.

Why do I need to check the oil?

Checking the engine oil is the one most important thing you can do to keep the car running smoothly. If the engine oil gets too low, the engine will wear more quickly, and you will soon have to splash out on an overhaul, or even a new engine.

Even a healthy engine will consume a little oil, so you'll almost certainly need to top up the oil once or twice between changes.

Some cars have an oil level gauge. These gauges only give an accurate reading when the car is parked on level ground and the ignition is switched on, before the engine is started. Once the engine is running, the gauge will not work.

The red oil warning light on the instrument panel is to warn that the engine oil pressure is low (due to a serious leak, very low oil level, or engine wear) – it is not an oil level warning light. If the oil warning light comes on when the engine is running, stop the engine immediately.

How do I check the oil?

You will need a wad of clean cloth, a pack of engine oil of the correct type (if you need to top up), and a funnel.

Before you start, park the car on level ground and make sure the engine has been stopped for at least five minutes.

1 Find the dipstick, and pull it right out of its tube. The top of the dipstick is often brightly coloured to help you find it.

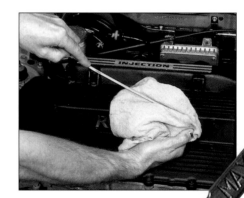

2 Wipe the oil off the dipstick using a clean cloth, and look for the oil level marks on the end of the dipstick.

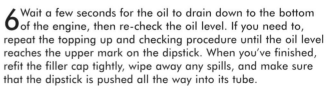

3 Push the dipstick slowly all the way back into its tube, then pull it out again. The level should be between the upper and lower marks.

4 If the level is near the lower mark, you need to top up. To top up, find the oil filler cap on top of the engine. There may also be filler caps for other systems, so if you're not sure, look in your car's handbook.

5 Remove the filler cap (some caps unscrew, while others are a push-fit), and pour in a little oil. Don't overfill the engine – it can cause leaks, and possibly damage.

6 Wait a few seconds for the oil to drain down to the bottom of the engine, then re-check the oil level. If you need to, repeat the topping up and checking procedure until the oil level reaches the upper mark on the dipstick. When you've finished, refit the filler cap tightly, wipe away any spills, and make sure that the dipstick is pushed all the way into its tube.

Why does my engine use so much oil?

It's normal to have to top up the engine oil once or twice between changes. On an old or high-mileage engine you might need to add up to a litre every thousand miles or so. If you find that you need to top up more often than this, there's almost certainly a problem.

The most common problem is a leak, which will show up as a black shiny mess on the engine and possibly as black drips where you park. Oil tends to run around the outside of the engine, making it hard to find the exact spot where the leak is

coming from. Check for signs of oil around the filter, and the drain plug (see "How to change the oil and filter"), and try retightening the filter or drain plug – don't overtighten, or this will cause a leak too! If there's no sign of leaks from the filter or drain plug, the oil is probably coming from one of the engine gaskets or oil seals – take the car to a garage to have it checked out.

The other way for the engine to lose oil is by burning it. The most obvious sign is blue smoke from the exhaust, especially when you start the engine from cold. If the engine is worn, sometimes the problem can be cured temporarily by using an engine oil additive, but the only long-term answer is an engine overhaul (it's often cheaper to fit an "exchange" rebuilt engine).

What else needs oil?

The engine isn't the only part of a car which needs oil. Other components which use oil are the transmission (refer to "The transmission") and, if fitted, the power steering system (refer to "Steering and suspension"). Always make sure that the correct type of oil is used for each component – using the wrong oil can cause serious damage.

The door hinges and locks should also be oiled frequently, using good quality general-

purpose oil. This will stop squeaks, corrosion and wear, and keep the components working smoothly. Don't use too much oil, it will find its way everywhere, including your clothes!

It's also a good idea to apply a little general-purpose oil to the pedal pivots, and any linkages (such as the throttle linkage) under the bonnet, if you can reach them. This will keep everything working like new, and will help to avoid any stiffness.

When does the oil need changing?

Oil deteriorates as the car is driven. It gets dirty and gradually loses its lubricating and cleaning properties. This causes wear inside the engine, and could be an expensive problem. If the oil is allowed to deteriorate too far, it forms black sludge which can block the engine oil passages, causing rapid wear and even engine failure. Not changing the oil regularly is definitely a false economy.

You can get some idea of the condition of the oil when you check the oil level on the dipstick. The oil does get blacker as it deteriorates, but this starts to happen within a few hundred miles of an oil change, so the colour of the oil is not a reliable guide to its condition. If the oil feels gritty when you rub a drop between your thumb and finger, or if it smells burnt, a change is overdue. Don't wait until you find black sludge on the end of the dipstick before you change the oil – your engine won't thank you!

The oil should be changed at the intervals recommended by your car manufacturer, or preferably more often. Consult your car's handbook for details. Most car manufacturers recommend that the oil is changed at intervals of between 6000 and 12,000 miles, but it's a good idea to do it more frequently if you can - certainly at no more than 6000 miles - regardless of what the manufacturer says. Bear in mind that oil also deteriorates with age, so you should always change the oil once a year, even if you do very few miles. You can't change the oil too often!

What does the filter do?

The filter catches small particles of dirt and metal in the oil, which could otherwise cause damage inside the engine.

Eventually, the filter starts to clog up and the oil can't flow through it as easily. If the filter clogs up completely, a bypass valve will open so that some oil can still reach the engine, but dirt and metal particles will be circulating as well - bad news!

A new filter should always be fitted whenever the engine oil is changed.

Always make sure that you buy the correct filter for your particular engine. Make a note of the engine size, and what year your car was registered, before going to buy a filter - this will help to make sure you get the right type. You can buy filters for most cars from good car accessory shops and motor factors.

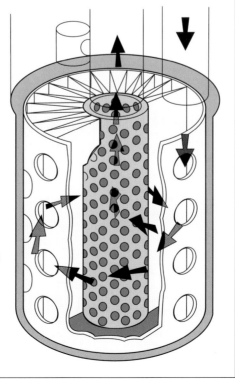

Leaks

Refer to "Why does my engine use so much oil?" and "Troubleshooting".

How to change the oil and filter

Changing the oil is one of the easiest jobs to do on a car, and you might want to do it yourself to save money. Why pay someone, when you can do the job yourself for less?

You will need plenty of clean cloth, disposable gloves, draining container (usually about 5 litres capacity), oil filter removal tool, spanner or drain plug key to fit the oil drain plug, new oil filter, new oil drain plug sealing washer, pack of engine oil of the correct type, and a funnel.

Before you start, the car should be parked on level ground and the engine should be warm (after a short run).

1 Remove the oil filler cap from the top of the engine. Find the oil drain plug in the sump underneath the engine. The oil will come out with some force at first, so position the draining container under the plug so the oil doesn't miss it!

2 Put on the gloves, and slacken the drain plug using the spanner or drain plug key. Unscrew it by hand the last couple of turns, keeping the plug pressed into its hole. When the plug comes out, pull it away quickly so the oil only runs into the container.

3 Allow about 10 minutes for the oil to drain. Wipe the drain plug clean. Remove the old sealing washer and fit the new one.

4 When the oil stops draining, wipe around the plug hole, then screw in the plug and tighten it. Make sure the plug's tight, but not too tight.

5 Now you need to find the oil filter, usually a cylindrical metal canister near the bottom of the engine, at the back, front or side. Check your car's handbook for details.

6 Use the oil filter removal tool to slacken the filter (turn it anti-clockwise). Once the filter is loose, unscrew it by hand. Drain the oil from inside the filter into the container.

7 Wipe clean around the filter mounting on the engine. Take the new oil filter, and smear a little clean engine oil on the rubber sealing ring.

8 Screw the new filter onto the engine by hand, until the sealing ring touches the engine, then tighten it by hand about another half- to three-quarters of a turn. Pull the draining container and tools out from under the car.

9 Check your car's handbook to see how much oil the engine needs, then pour in about two-thirds of the recommended quantity through the filler hole at the top of the engine. Use a funnel to stop spills.

10 Wait a few minutes for the oil to drain down into the engine, then pull out the dipstick and check the oil level (see "How do I check the oil?").

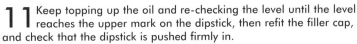

11 Keep topping up the oil and re-checking the level until the level reaches the upper mark on the dipstick, then refit the filler cap, and check that the dipstick is pushed firmly in.

12 Start the engine. The red oil pressure warning light on the dashboard will take a few seconds to go out (if it doesn't go out, stop the engine!). Run the engine for a few minutes, and check for leaks around the oil filter and drain plug. Re-tighten slightly if necessary, but don't overtighten.

13 Stop the engine and wait a few minutes for the oil to run down into the engine again, then re-check the oil level. Top up if necessary, but don't overfill. Pour the old oil into a container, and take it to your local oil recycling centre (most garages have a waste tank, and will probably take the oil for you if you ask). Don't pour the oil down a drain or into the ground!

That's it – easy wasn't it!

What sort of oil do I need?

Although all oils might look similar, there are different types and grades, all designed for different tasks, so it's important that the oil you use meets the specifications recommended by your car manufacturer.

First, check your car's handbook to see what type of oil the manufacturer recommends. Sometimes, the recommended oil type is marked on the engine, or on one of the body panels under the bonnet. Often a range of oils is recommended, depending on the temperature range the car is likely to be used in.

The two main things to look out for in the oil specification are the viscosity (thickness) grade shown by the "SAE" rating, and the quality (indicated by the "API" or "ACEA" rating). These specifications will be marked on the oil packaging, and most well-known brands will be suitable – if the packaging doesn't have any specifications marked on it, don't buy it!

Another thing to consider is what type of oil you're going to use. The cheaper oils are usually "mineral-based", the mid-price oils usually "semi-synthetic" and the expensive oils "fully-synthetic". The more expensive, synthetic oils give better protection but are only really needed in very high-performance engines or cars. The mineral-based oils give enough protection for most normal engines.

Technical Information

SAE 15W/40
Mineral formula
Oil Colour: Green

Meets requirements of:
API SG/SH/SJ,CCMC G4,
ACEA A3-96

All about fuel

For most people, fuel is the biggest single out-of-pocket expense involved in running a car. Unless you're about to change cars you don't have much choice in what fuel you buy, but you can usually save a little by choosing where to buy it. This chapter explains the pros and cons of the various fuels available – petrol, diesel, LPG and electricity – and gives some tips on getting the best possible fuel consumption. There is also some advice on what to do if you accidentally put the wrong fuel into your car's tank, although the best advice of all for that situation is – don't do it!

Different types of fuel

There are two main types of fuel for cars, petrol and diesel (see "The engine"). There are a few alternative fuels, including LPG (Liquefied Petroleum Gas), and even electricity, but at present they're not in widespread use.

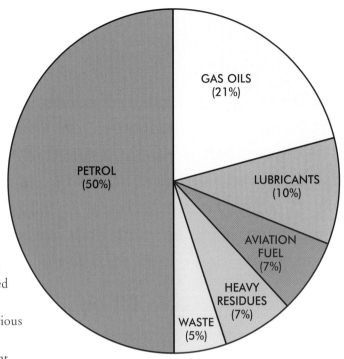

FRACTIONAL YIELDS OF CRUDE OIL

Petrol and diesel fuel are produced from crude oil. Because petrol is now such an important fuel, the amount of petrol obtained from one barrel of crude oil has gone up significantly from the days when crude oil was first discovered. It's now possible to get nearly half a barrel of petrol from one barrel of crude oil – half of the crude oil produced is used to make petrol!

Once petrol and diesel fuel have been refined from crude oil, they're treated with various additives and detergents to make them suitable for use in car engines.

The reserves of natural crude oil are beginning to run out, and it's widely believed that they'll be exhausted completely within the next few decades. Most car manufacturers are trying to build more fuel-efficient engines, in an attempt to eke out the oil reserves for longer.

Details of how an engine burns petrol and diesel are given in "The engine".

Petrol

In recent years, it's been realised that petrol engine exhaust fumes cause a significant pollution problem throughout the world. Car engines must now be fitted with systems to cut down harmful exhaust emissions, and the petrol itself must be "cleaner". In many countries, all new cars must run on "unleaded" petrol, which is more environmentally-friendly than "leaded" petrol.

Diesel

Diesel cars are more fuel efficient. Diesel engines produce less harmful exhaust gas emissions than petrol engines, although they produce more smoke particles.

Liquefied Petroleum Gas (LPG)

LPG is a mixture of liquefied petroleum gases, which are obtained from crude oil. LPG is stored as a liquid in a pressurised container, and is released to form a vapour before it's burnt by the engine. Although a conventional combustion engine is used (similar to a petrol engine – see "The engine"), a special pressurised fuel tank, and modified fuel system components are fitted.

An engine running on LPG is less fuel efficient than a similar engine running on petrol, but the exhaust emissions are much cleaner.

Because LPG is produced from crude oil, sources of LPG are likely to run out, so although LPG is more environmentally-friendly, it isn't a long-term alternative.

Electricity

An electric car is fitted with a number of batteries to drive an electric motor, which powers the car.

Although electric cars themselves cause very little pollution, and are cheap to run, at the moment the batteries used are very heavy and need to be recharged often – this means that electric cars can travel relatively small distances between "refuelling" (recharging) stops. The power stations which produce the electricity may also be causing pollution, so the electric car may not be as "green" as it first seems.

Most of the large car manufacturers are carrying out research into electric cars, to improve their performance and practicality, so they should become more widespread in the future.

Filling up

Although we all routinely fill our cars up with fuel without a great deal of concern, it's potentially a very dangerous job. When you fill up with petrol, vapour is released, which when mixed with the surrounding air, can form a highly explosive mixture. The biggest risks when filling up come from naked flames and sparks, and accidental spillage.

Why do I have to fill up so often?

Apart from an obvious leak, the biggest influence on fuel consumption is driving style – heavy acceleration, braking, and frequent gear-changing all use more fuel. Basically, the smoother the driving style, the more economical it will be.

Poorly adjusted or faulty fuel system components can cause high consumption, and if you think there may be a problem, it's worth taking the car to a garage to have it checked.

To decide whether your car's fuel consumption is high, first of all, you need to have realistic expectations of what the consumption should be. Don't be surprised if your car doesn't meet the manufacturer's quoted fuel consumption figures – these figures are often recorded in controlled tests, simulating "normal" driving conditions.

Here's a quick guide to help you calculate fuel consumption. If you repeat this calculation for a few tankfuls of fuel, you'll get a more accurate idea of the overall consumption.

When you're filling up, there are a few safety precautions which you must take by law . . .

NO SMOKING, and don't use a mobile phone whilst you're filling up

Don't be surprised if your fuel consumption figures vary quite a lot. If you take your car on a long trip travelling, the consumption is often different to when you're covering a similar overall mileage driving a few miles to and from work. You might even find that the consumption varies from season to season.

If you find that your fuel consumption is higher than normal, and you can't find any other explanation, there may be a leak somewhere. If you think there's a leak, don't drive the car (refer to "Leaks").

1. Fill your fuel tank, and zero the trip meter on the dashboard
2. Don't fill up again until your fuel gauge registers nearly empty
3. Read off the mileage on the trip meter before filling up
4. Make a note of exactly how much fuel you put in
5. You can now work out the fuel consumption as follows:

$$\frac{\text{Mileage covered}}{\text{Amount of fuel}} = \text{Fuel consumption}$$

So if you needed 10 gallons to fill up, and you had covered 420 miles since the last fill-up:

$$\frac{\text{Mileage covered} = 420}{\text{Amount of fuel} = 10} = 42 \text{ miles per gallon (mpg)}$$

Leaded and lead replacement petrol

Leaded petrol will not be available anywhere in the EC from January 2000. A substitute known as "lead replacement petrol" (LRP) will be sold at the pumps. Anti-wear additives for use with unleaded petrol will also be available.

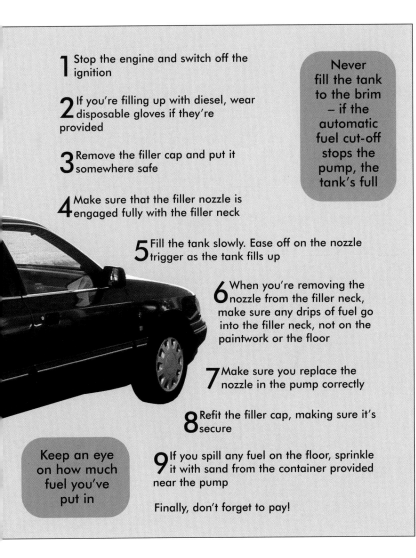

1 Stop the engine and switch off the ignition

2 If you're filling up with diesel, wear disposable gloves if they're provided

3 Remove the filler cap and put it somewhere safe

4 Make sure that the filler nozzle is engaged fully with the filler neck

5 Fill the tank slowly. Ease off on the nozzle trigger as the tank fills up

6 When you're removing the nozzle from the filler neck, make sure any drips of fuel go into the filler neck, not on the paintwork or the floor

7 Make sure you replace the nozzle in the pump correctly

8 Refit the filler cap, making sure it's secure

9 If you spill any fuel on the floor, sprinkle it with sand from the container provided near the pump

Finally, don't forget to pay!

> Never fill the tank to the brim – if the automatic fuel cut-off stops the pump, the tank's full

> Keep an eye on how much fuel you've put in

Problems with petrol

Any problems with petrol are usually due to contamination, which can cause engine running problems. If you think the petrol may be contaminated, see if the problem is still there after you next fill up - if it is, have the fuel system checked.

Most cars that can run only on unleaded petrol have a small fuel filler neck – the wrong pump nozzle won't fit, so you can't fill up with the wrong fuel!

What to do if you fill up with the wrong fuel

Unleaded instead of leaded petrol

If you've just put a few litres of unleaded petrol in the tank, stop filling with unleaded, move to the leaded pump, and carry on filling with leaded petrol. You won't have any problems.

If you've filled the tank with unleaded petrol, drive the car until the fuel tank is about half empty, then fill the tank again with leaded petrol.

Diesel instead of petrol

Don't try to start the engine – if you do, it won't run for long, and you'll need to have all the fuel system components thoroughly cleaned and checked!

You'll need to have the fuel tank drained, cleaned and refilled with petrol before you can drive the car – call for help.

Petrol instead of diesel

If you've just put a few litres of petrol in the tank, stop filling with petrol, move to the diesel pump, and carry on filling with diesel. You won't have any problems.

If you've filled the tank with petrol, don't try to start the engine – if you do, it won't run for long, and you'll need to have all the fuel system components thoroughly cleaned and checked, which could be expensive!

You'll need to have the fuel tank drained, cleaned and refilled with diesel before you can drive the car – call for help.

Problems with diesel

Problems are usually associated with cold weather, or with water contamination.

Cold weather problems

Diesel sold in cold conditions is different to that sold when the weather's warmer. This is because diesel fuel goes "waxy" when it gets cold, and can even freeze - additives are used in cold weather to try to reduce problems.

Most diesel engine cars have a fuel heater, which warms the fuel before it goes into the engine – this normally stops problems in cold weather.

If you do have problems due to fuel waxing, the only thing you can do is warm the engine, or wait for the weather to warm up – never use a naked flame to warm an engine. The best solution is to park the car in a garage, and use an electric heater to warm the engine.

Water in fuel

Diesel cars usually have a water separator, and one of the regular maintenance jobs is to drain off the water – if water gets into the fuel system, it can cause corrosion. Make sure that you drain off water from the separator at the recommended intervals, or more often if necessary – this will avoid problems (see "Fluids and filters").

Leaks

Never drive the car if you think there may be a fuel leak – leaking fuel, or fuel vapour could be ignited by the hot exhaust or engine components, which can cause a rapid and serious fire or even an explosion.

Refer to "Troubleshooting" for details of what to do if you think there might be a fuel leak.

Fluids and filters

All cars rely on various fluids and filters to operate safely and efficiently. You can think of the fluids as a car's blood supply – if the fluids deteriorate, or leak, it's likely to cause problems! Filters are used to remove dirt and other contamination from the fluids, from the air drawn into the engine (air filter) or the car's interior (pollen filter).

To prevent any problems, all the fluids should be checked regularly, and the fluids and filter should always be renewed at the intervals recommended by the manufacturers.

What should I check and when?

We've given a guide to the mileage and time interval for each check, but this is only a guide, and you should always follow the manufacturer's recommendations. Sometimes the manufacturer may recommend that the checks are carried out at longer intervals than given here, and sometimes at shorter intervals. Bear in mind that some of the fluids and filters deteriorate with age, so you should always carry out the checks or changes at the recommended time intervals even if you cover very few miles. Basically, you can't carry out these checks too often, but if you don't carry them out often enough, you may have problems.

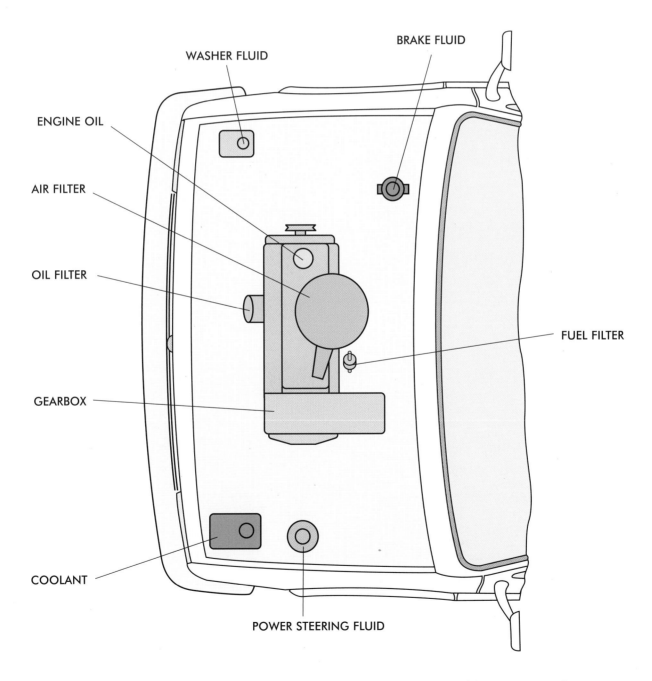

WASHER FLUID

BRAKE FLUID

ENGINE OIL

AIR FILTER

OIL FILTER

FUEL FILTER

GEARBOX

COOLANT

POWER STEERING FLUID

TYPICAL ENGINE COMPARTMENT FLUIDS AND FILTERS

Engine oil and oil filter

If the engine oil level gets too low, it could cause serious engine damage, so it's vital to check the oil level regularly. Check the engine oil level once a week, or before a long journey.

The engine oil and filter should be renewed at the manufacturer's recommended intervals (normally at least every 6000 miles or 12 months).

Refer to "All about oil" for details of oil renewal.

Brake fluid

If the brake fluid level gets too low, the brakes will work poorly, or not at all. Regular checking of the fluid level will warn you if a leak's developing. The fluid level falls gradually as the brake pads wear, but if you're topping up regularly, there must be a leak – stop driving the car until the leak's been found and fixed.

Check the brake fluid level once a week, or before a long journey.

The fluid should be renewed every 12 months, regardless of mileage. **Note:** Some Citroën cars do not use the same type of fluid – see "LHM fluid (certain Citroën cars)".

1 Make sure the car is level, then wipe the brake fluid reservoir clean. The level must be kept between the "MAX" and "MIN" marks.

2 If topping up is needed, unscrew and remove the reservoir cap. Usually, the inside of the cap fits down into the fluid, so pull it out slowly, and place it on a piece of clean cloth to catch drips.

3 Top up to the "MAX" mark. Use a good quality brake fluid which meets the standard DOT 4 (this will be marked on the container). Always use new fluid from a freshly-opened container.

4 Refit the reservoir cap and discard the cloth.

WARNING

Brake fluid is poisonous. It's also flammable, and acts as a very effective paint stripper. Wash any splashes off skin or paintwork right away with lots of clean water.

Coolant

The coolant is pumped around the engine, and cools it by means of the radiator. If the level gets too low, it could cause overheating and serious engine damage. It's normal to have to top up occasionally, but the need for regular topping-up suggests that there's a leak or some other problem which should be fixed before it gets serious. Make sure you use the right type of coolant for topping up – some cars use coolant which cannot be mixed with other types (check in your car's handbook for details).

Check the level once a week, or before a long journey. The coolant should be renewed at the manufacturer's recommended intervals. A few manufacturers use "lifetime" coolant, which is designed to last the life of the car – check in your car's handbook for details.

The coolant reservoir may be transparent, or it may have a level indicator inside, which is visible once the cap has been removed.

1 Check the level is up to the relevant mark (or between the "MIN" and "MAX" marks). If you need to remove the reservoir cap, carefully unscrew the cap and check the level.

2 If the level's low, top up using a 50/50 mixture of water and antifreeze (or clean tap water in an emergency) to bring the level up to the appropriate mark. Don't overfill.

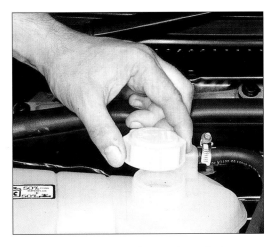

3 Refit the cap tightly afterwards, and wipe away any spillage.

WARNING

Never undo the reservoir cap while the engine is hot – danger of scalding. Unscrew the cap slowly and allow any pressure to escape. Wash off any accidental splashes from the skin, and from the car's bodywork – it can cause paint damage.

Power steering fluid

If your car has power steering and the fluid level's low, there may be a hissing or squealing sound as the steering wheel is turned. If the level is very low, or the system's leaking, the power steering system may be damaged, and the steering wheel will be harder to turn.

Most power steering systems use automatic transmission fluid, but you should always check with your car's handbook – different types of system use different fluids, and you could cause damage if you use the wrong fluid. Have the system checked for leaks if you need to top up regularly.

Check the power steering fluid level once a week, or before a long journey.

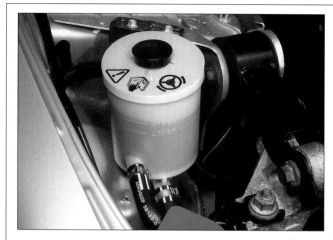

The power steering fluid reservoir may be transparent with level markings on the outside, or it may have a level dipstick fitted to the filler cap.

1 If you need to remove the filler cap to check the level, wipe around the cap first, then unscrew the cap.

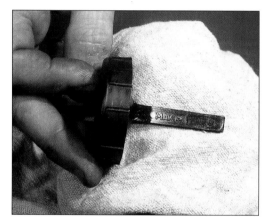

2 Read off the fluid level, and top up if necessary. Sometimes there may be "HOT" and "COLD" level markings for use depending on whether the engine's hot or cold – the level should be up to the relevant mark.

3 If the level's low, wipe around the filler cap, then remove it, if not already done, and top up to the correct mark. Don't overfill. Refit the filler cap tightly afterwards.

Screenwash

You can use plain water in the washer reservoir, but using a good quality screenwash additive will help clean the screen, and its anti-icing properties are essential in winter to stop the washer jets freezing up. Note the directions on the container as to the quantity to add.

Check the screenwash fluid level once a week, or before a long journey. Many people find it convenient to top up the screenwash fluid when they fill up with fuel.

The windscreen washer reservoir is usually located in the engine compartment. If your car is fitted with headlight washers, the headlight washers normally use fluid from the windscreen washer fluid reservoir, although on some cars a separate reservoir may be fitted. Similarly, if a tailgate washer system is fitted, there may be a combined windscreen/tailgate fluid reservoir, or there may be a separate tailgate washer fluid reservoir (sometimes in the boot).

1 If you need to top up, wipe away any dirt from around the filler neck, then pull off the filler cap.

2 Fill the reservoir, then refit the cap firmly, and wipe away any spillage. A funnel can make it easier to top up.

3 You can clear a blocked washer jet by poking the fine nozzle gently with a pin. You can also use the pin to swivel the "eyeball" so that the jet is aimed correctly – but don't break the pin off in the nozzle.

WARNING

Never use engine antifreeze in the washer system – it's not only hazardous to health, but it will also damage the car's paintwork and trim. Use a good quality screenwash additive/de-icer.

Manual transmission oil

If the oil level gets low, the transmission may become noisy, and you might have trouble selecting gears. (Note though that gear selection trouble can also be caused by clutch problems – see "The transmission"). If the level gets too low, the transmission may be damaged. There are several different types of oil, and it's essential that you use the right one, so you'll need to check with your car manufacturer's information, or an authorised dealer.

The oil level should be checked at the manufacturer's recommended intervals (usually around every 12,000 miles or 12 months), but note that some cars have "sealed-for-life" transmissions, and there's no way of checking the oil level. You should also have the oil level checked if you suspect that there's a leak.

On some cars the transmission oil should be renewed at the manufacturer's recommended intervals – often around every 60,000 miles. Check your car's handbook, or check with an authorised dealer for details.

Make sure you unscrew the correct bolts – check with the car's handbook or a dealer.

Checking and renewing the transmission oil can be tricky, so you might want to have the work done by a suitably-equipped garage.

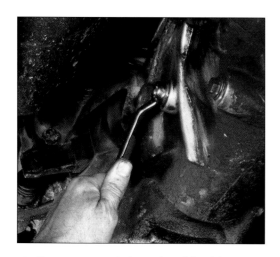

1 On most transmissions, the oil level is checked using a level hole in the side of the transmission casing. First of all, you need to make sure that the car's on level ground. To check the level, the level plug is unscrewed from the transmission – often the plug can only be reached from under the car. Have a container ready to catch any spillage.

2 Usually, the oil level should be up to the bottom edge of the level plug hole, but on a few transmissions the level should be a specified distance below. If the oil level needs to be topped up, it's usually done through the level plug hole.

3 Sometimes topping-up is done through a filler hole in the top of the transmission casing. Wipe away any spills, and refit the level plug and, where applicable, the filler plug.

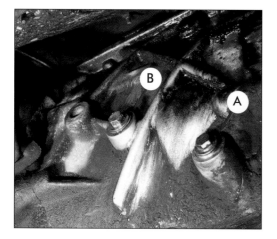

4 To renew the transmission oil, a drain plug is usually found near the bottom of the transmission. Place a container under the transmission, then unscrew the drain plug (A), and the level plug (B), and allow the oil to drain. When all the oil has drained, refit and tighten the drain plug, and top up through the level or filler hole.

Automatic transmission fluid

If the automatic transmission fluid level gets low, the transmission may not work properly – low fluid level is a common source of problems with automatic transmissions. If the level gets too low, it could damage the transmission. There are several different types of transmission fluid, and it's essential that you use the right one, so you'll need to check with your car manufacturer's information, or an authorised dealer. If frequent topping-up is needed, have the cause found and fixed without delay.

The automatic transmission fluid should be checked at the manufacturer's recommended intervals (at least every 6000 miles or 12 months).

The following advice is only a guide - you need to check your car's handbook to see exactly how to check the automatic transmission fluid level, but most use the same technique, with a level dipstick which fits inside a tube attached to the transmission. The level is usually checked with the transmission warm, after a short drive.

Have the transmission oil renewed at the manufacturer's recommended intervals (usually around every 30,000 miles).

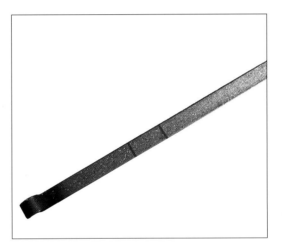

1 With the engine running and the handbrake on, press the brake pedal, and move the gear selector lever through all the gear positions, starting and ending in "P". Let the engine idle for one minute then, with the engine still running, pull out the dipstick. Wipe the dipstick with a clean cloth, and push it carefully back into its tube.

2 Pull out the dipstick again then check the fluid level. Often, you'll find the dipstick has two sets of markings, one for checking the fluid hot (or at high temperature, eg, 80°C), and one for checking cold (or at low temperature, eg, 20°C).

3 Read off the fluid level, and if topping-up is needed, stop the engine.

4 Usually, topping-up is done through the dipstick tube, so you'll need a bottle with a tube, or a clean funnel, to stop spills. Don't overfill, and be very careful not to introduce dust or dirt into the transmission.

5 Re-check the level with the engine running, and finally refit the dipstick when the level's correct.

Clutch fluid

Some cars with manual transmission have a hydraulic clutch. Sometimes, the clutch hydraulic system may be sealed, or may share a common reservoir with the braking system – alternatively, there may be a separate clutch fluid reservoir (check your car's handbook for details). If the fluid needs topping-up, there must be a leak – a bad leak will stop the clutch working, so have the system checked if you need to top up regularly.

Check the clutch fluid level once a week, or before a long journey.

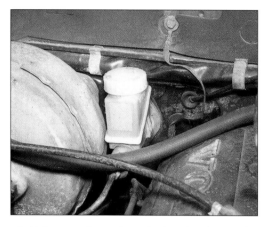

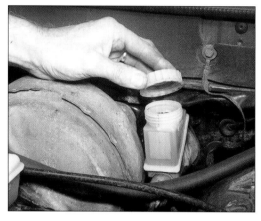

1 Make sure the car's parked on level ground, then wipe the clutch fluid reservoir clean if it's dirty. The fluid level must always be kept between the "MAX" and "MIN" marks – if there are no level markings, the fluid level should normally be up to the lower edge of the reservoir filler neck.

2 If topping-up is needed, unscrew and remove the reservoir cap.

3 Top up using new brake fluid. Use a good quality brake fluid which meets the standard DOT 4 (this will be marked on the container). Always use new fluid from a freshly-opened container - using old brake fluid could result in the clutch not working properly.

4 Refit the reservoir cap when you've finished.

WARNING

Hydraulic fluid is poisonous. It's also flammable, and acts as a very effective paint stripper. Wash any splashes off skin or paintwork right away with lots of clean water.

Rear final drive oil

On rear-wheel-drive cars, if the final drive oil level gets low, the final drive (differential) may become noisy. If the level gets very low, the differential may be damaged. (On front-wheel-drive cars, the final drive is integral with the transmission.)

There are several different types of final drive oil, so you'll need to check with your car manufacturer's information, or an authorised dealer.

The final drive oil level should be checked at the manufacturer's recommended intervals (typically around every 12,000 miles or 12 months, although some manufacturers don't specify a level check). You should also check the level if the back axle becomes noisy (whining or rumbling noises), or if there's evidence of oil leakage (oily areas on the back axle or oil droppings under the back of the car).

On some cars, the final drive oil should be renewed at the manufacturer's recommended intervals – often around 60,000 miles. On other cars, there's no need to renew the oil. Check your car's handbook, or with an authorised dealer for details.

Checking and renewing the final drive oil can be tricky, so you might want to have the work done by a suitably-equipped garage.

On most final drives, the oil level is checked using a level hole in the final drive casing. If you're unscrewing the level plug, have a container ready to catch any spillage.

1 First of all, you need to make sure that the car's on level ground. To check the level, the level plug is unscrewed from the final drive – often the plug can only be reached from under the car.

2 Usually, the oil level should be up to the bottom edge of the level plug hole – check your car's handbook, or ask an authorised dealer to make sure.

3 If the oil level needs to be topped up, it's done through the level plug hole. Top up until the oil reaches the bottom of the level plug hole.

4 Wipe away any spills, and refit the level plug.

5 To renew the final drive oil, a drain plug is usually provided near the bottom of the final drive. Place a container under the final drive unit, then unscrew the drain plug, and the level plug (as described previously), and allow the oil to drain. When all the oil has drained, refit and tighten the drain plug, and top up through the level hole.

Air filter

The filter stops dirt and dust from being sucked into the engine. If the element's very dirty or blocked, the engine won't run properly, and the fuel consumption might be higher than normal. If the filter is missing or split, dirt may be sucked into the engine, causing expensive damage. When buying a new air filter, you'll need to know the model, engine size and year of manufacture of your car.

Renew the air filter at the manufacturer's recommended intervals, typically every 24,000 miles or two years.

Air filters are usually housed in a rectangular casing next to the engine, or a round casing on top of the engine. Sometimes you may have to unclip a hose or disconnect a wiring plug before you can remove the air filter cover.

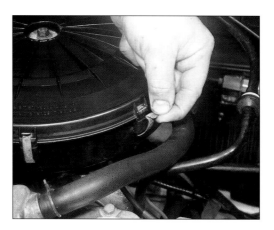

1 Release the clips and/or unscrew the securing screws, then lift the cover from the air filter housing.

2 Lift out the air filter, noting which way up it's fitted (some filters fit either way up). Make sure the new filter's the same.

3 Wipe out the casing and the cover using a clean cloth. Be careful not to get any dirt or dust into the air intake.

4 Fit the new filter into the housing, making sure that it's the right way up, then refit the cover and secure it with the clips and/or screws.

LHM fluid (certain Citroën cars)

Certain Citroën cars use a hydraulic system to control the suspension, brakes and power steering. This system uses a special hydraulic fluid (LHM). As with any hydraulic system, a need for frequent topping-up can only be due to a leak, which should be found and fixed without delay.

The LHM fluid level should be checked every week, or before a long journey, and the fluid should be renewed every 36,000 miles. Renewing the fluid can be a tricky job, and it's best to get it done by a suitably-equipped garage.

To check the LHM hydraulic fluid level, first start the engine, and with the engine idling, set the suspension height control lever inside the car to the "Maximum" position.

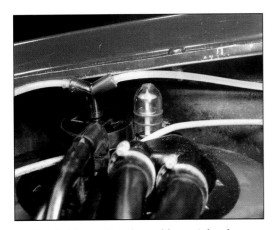

1 The fluid level is indicated by a sight glass on top of the fluid reservoir in the engine compartment. The level indicator float should be between the two rings on the sight glass – the level indication is only accurate when the car has stabilised at its maximum height.

2 If you need to top up, use clean LHM fluid. Remove the filler cap on top of the fluid reservoir, and top up until the level indicator float is between the two rings. When the level's correct, refit the reservoir cap, and stop the engine.

> ### WARNING
> The fluid used in Citroën hydraulic systems is LHM mineral fluid, which is green in colour. The use of any other type of fluid, including normal brake fluid, will damage the system rubber seals and hoses. Keep the LHM fluid sealed in its original container. Note that most Citroën cars with conventional suspension (springs and shock absorbers instead of hydraulics) use conventional brake hydraulic fluid in the braking system, and automatic transmission fluid in the power steering system – don't use LHM fluid in these systems.

Fuel filter – diesel engines

The fuel filter stops any dirt in the fuel from getting into the fuel injection system. The dirt could otherwise cause blockages, which would make the engine run badly, or not at all, and possibly cause expensive damage. After a period of time, the filter will become full of dirt, and the fuel won't pass through it properly. To prevent problems, the filter must be renewed at the recommended intervals.

As well as filtering out dirt, most fuel filter assemblies incorporate a water separator to prevent any water in the fuel from getting into the fuel system components. The water can be drained off from the filter using a drain plug.

Water should be drained from the fuel filter assembly at least every 6000 miles or 6 months, or as soon as the "water in fuel" warning light (if fitted) comes on. It should also be drained at the beginning of winter in order to avoid problems caused by the water freezing.

The fuel filter should be renewed at the manufacturer's recommended intervals (typically around every 18,000 miles).

To drain off water, a drain plug is usually provided at the bottom of the fuel filter housing. Place a suitable container under the drain plug or tube, then slacken the plug, and allow fuel and water to drain until fuel, free from water, emerges. Close the drain plug, then dispose of the drained fuel safely.

1 The method of filter renewal varies, so it's best to check your car's handbook for details, or ask a suitably-equipped garage to do the job.

2 If you need to disconnect any fuel pipes, make a note before you disconnect them so that you can reconnect the pipes correctly. Take suitable precautions, because fuel will almost certainly be spilt.

3 When the filter's been changed, the fuel system will have to be primed. Usually, there's a priming button or a rubber priming bulb fitted in the fuel line to the fuel filter to draw fuel up from the fuel tank to prime the fuel system – check your car's handbook for details.

WARNING

Diesel fuel is irritating to the skin. Wear disposable gloves or use barrier cream.

Fuel filter – petrol engines

Some older cars don't have a fuel filter, but all modern cars, and all cars with fuel injection, do. The fuel filter stops any dirt in the fuel from getting into the fuel system. The dirt could otherwise cause blockages, which would make the engine run badly, or not at all, and possibly cause expensive damage. After a period of time, the filter will become full of dirt, and the fuel won't pass through it properly. To prevent problems, the filter must be renewed at the recommended intervals.

The fuel filter should be renewed at the manufacturer's recommended intervals (usually around every 60,000 miles).

Because it's necessary to disconnect fuel pipes to renew the fuel filter, it's best to get a suitably-equipped garage to renew the filter for you.

WARNING

Fuel pipes may contain fuel under pressure. Don't attempt to disconnect fuel pipes unless you're quite sure you know what you're doing.

Pollen filter

Some cars are fitted with a pollen filter to filter the air which goes into the heating/ventilation system. The filter will stop pollen and dust from the atmosphere being drawn into the car's interior.

The pollen filter should be renewed at the manufacturer's recommended intervals (usually around 20,000 miles or 2 years).

1 Pollen filters come in various shapes and sizes, and you might have to remove surrounding trim panels for access to the filter.

2 Pollen filters are usually located under the scuttle panel at the back of the engine compartment, or behind the facia, inside the car.

The engine

The internal combustion engine has had a profound effect on almost every aspect of 20th century life. If the designers of the first engines were able to examine the engines of today, they might be surprised at how little has changed. Certainly, modern materials and computer technology have made engines lighter, quieter and much more efficient, but the mechanical components at the heart of the engine have not changed much.

This chapter explains how the engine works, how to keep it healthy and what to do if it seems to be going wrong. If you've ever wondered what a timing belt does or how a catalytic converter works, you'll find the answers here. There's also some practical advice on simple DIY tasks like fitting new spark plugs and checking drivebelts.

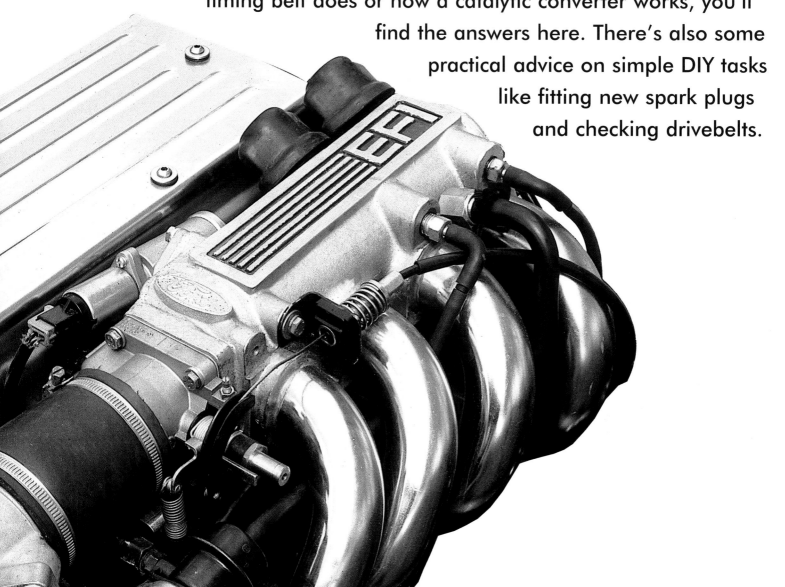

How does it work?

The engine is a machine which converts chemical energy (hydrocarbons in the fuel) into mechanical energy in the form of motion. It does this by burning fuel inside its cylinders – hence the term "internal combustion engine".

Fuel/air mixture is drawn into a cylinder, and the mixture is compressed by a piston and burnt. When the mixture burns, it expands very quickly and pushes the piston down the cylinder.

The piston is connected to the crankshaft by a connecting rod which pushes the crankshaft round. The crankshaft is connected to the transmission, which drives the car's wheels.

Inlet and exhaust valves at the top of the cylinder allow the fuel/air mixture into the cylinder, and burnt gases out into the exhaust system. The valves are opened and closed by a camshaft, which is driven from the crankshaft, usually by a timing belt or timing chain.

In a four-stroke engine, the piston moves up and down twice (two up-strokes, and two down-strokes, making four strokes), to produce one pulse of power. The four strokes are:

a) *Intake* – the piston moves down, sucking fuel/air mixture into the cylinder via the inlet valve.

b) *Compression* – the valves are closed and the piston moves up, compressing the mixture until it's ignited at the top of the stroke.

c) *Power* – the piston is pushed down as the burning mixture expands.

d) *Exhaust* – the piston moves back up the cylinder (due to the momentum produced during the power stroke), and the burnt gases are pushed out through the open exhaust valve. The cycle then starts again, with another intake stroke.

On petrol engines the fuel/air mixture is ignited by a spark from the spark plug (see "Spark plugs").

On diesel engines the inlet valve lets air into the cylinder; the fuel is injected straight into the cylinder by a fuel injector (fuel is pumped to the injector by a fuel injection pump). When the fuel/air mixture is compressed, the temperature rises very quickly, and the mixture ignites by itself.

THE FOUR-STROKE CYCLE

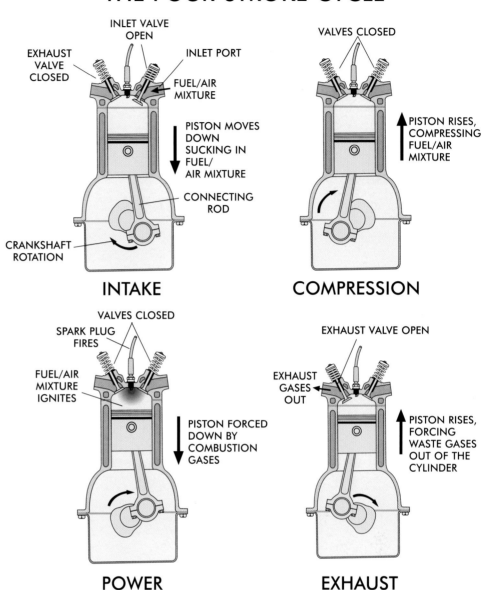

INTAKE

COMPRESSION

POWER

EXHAUST

Multi-valve engines

Most older car engines have one inlet valve and one exhaust valve per cylinder – ie, two valves per cylinder. Many modern engines have three, four, or in a few cases even five valves per cylinder, although the most common configuration is four valves per cylinder. Such an engine has two inlet valves and two exhaust valves for each cylinder (so a four-cylinder engine would be a "16-valve" engine).

Using multiple valves gives improved efficiency, because they allow the fuel/air mixture to enter the cylinder, and the exhaust gases to leave, more easily.

Double-overhead-camshaft engines

Double-overhead-camshaft (or "twin-cam") engines have two camshafts, one operating the exhaust valves, and one operating the inlet valves. Multi-valve engines are almost always double-overhead-camshaft engines.

How to avoid problems

Modern engines are very reliable, and if you look after the engine, you shouldn't have any problems. If something does go wrong however, here are a few tips to help you find what's causing the trouble.

Petrol (or diesel)

Always keep the fuel tank topped up, and make sure you use the correct type of fuel. If you run out of fuel, dirt or sediment from the bottom of the fuel tank can be drawn into the fuel system, and although most cars have a fuel filter, blockages or contamination from very fine particles can still cause trouble. For details of other possible fuel problems, refer to "All about fuel".

Oil

Check the oil level regularly, and renew the oil and filter at the recommended intervals (make sure you use the correct type of oil for your engine). Oil is the engine's blood supply - without oil, the engine will die! If the oil pressure warning light on the dashboard comes on, stop the engine immediately. Refer to "All about oil" for more details.

Electricity

Make sure the battery is in good condition, and check all the engine electrical connections. Electrical problems are amongst the most common causes of breakdowns. Refer to "Electrical things" for more details.

Coolant

Check the coolant level regularly, and keep it topped up. If you've got a leak, have it fixed as soon as possible. Keep an eye on the temperature gauge, and if the engine overheats, stop and let it cool down before continuing your journey. Overheating can cause serious engine damage. Refer to "Cooling and heating" for more details.

Rubber – hoses and drivebelts

Check all the engine's rubber hoses for damage and deterioration, and make sure all the hose clips are tight - leaking hoses can cause serious problems. Regularly check the engine auxiliary drivebelt(s) and, where applicable, have the engine timing belt renewed at the intervals recommended by the manufacturer (normally around every 36,000 miles) – refer to "Drivebelts" for more details.

DO'S AND DON'TS TO KEEP YOUR ENGINE IN TIP-TOP CONDITION

DO check the engine oil level every week, and before a long journey.

DO change the engine oil and filter at the intervals shown in your car's handbook, or more often if you can afford to.

DO check the coolant level and the drivebelt(s) regularly.

DO take the car out for a long run occasionally, if you normally only use it for short journeys.

DO stop immediately if the oil pressure warning light comes on when you're driving – it's not an oil level warning light, and you'll wreck the engine if you don't stop very quickly!

DON'T warm the engine up by leaving the car parked with the engine running – it's better just to start the engine and drive off straight away, even in winter.

DON'T warm the engine up by revving it more than normal.

DON'T rev the engine more than you need to until the temperature gauge has reached its normal position.

DON'T carry on driving the car if you know the engine is overheating.

Tuning up

A tune-up means that the engine fuel and ignition system settings are checked to make sure that they're within the manufacturer's recommended limits. On older cars, a garage can check, and if necessary adjust, the engine idle speed, the fuel/air mixture and the ignition timing, but on most modern cars, these settings are controlled by the engine management system, and can't be adjusted (although they can still be checked if the right equipment is available).

When carrying out a tune-up, it's also a good idea to carry out all the checks which should be done on the engine when the car is serviced.

Provided your car is regularly serviced, tuning up isn't very often needed on a modern car, because there's not much to go wrong.

These are the main checks which are normally done:

- Check the engine oil level
- Check the coolant level
- Check the air filter
- Check the fuel filter (where applicable)
- Check the spark plugs (petrol engines)
- Check the battery
- Check the ignition and fuel system wiring and hoses
- A garage may be able to check the engine idle speed, the fuel mixture and the ignition timing, but on most modern engines, these settings are controlled by the engine management system, and can't be adjusted.

Ignition and fuel systems

The ignition system creates the sparks which are used to ignite the fuel/air mixture on a petrol engine (diesel engines don't have an ignition system). The ignition coil uses low voltage electricity from the battery to produce the high-voltage electricity which is sent along the HT (High Tension) leads to the spark plugs. The spark plugs produce sparks inside the cylinders (see "Spark plugs").

The fuel system controls the amount of fuel and air burnt by the engine.

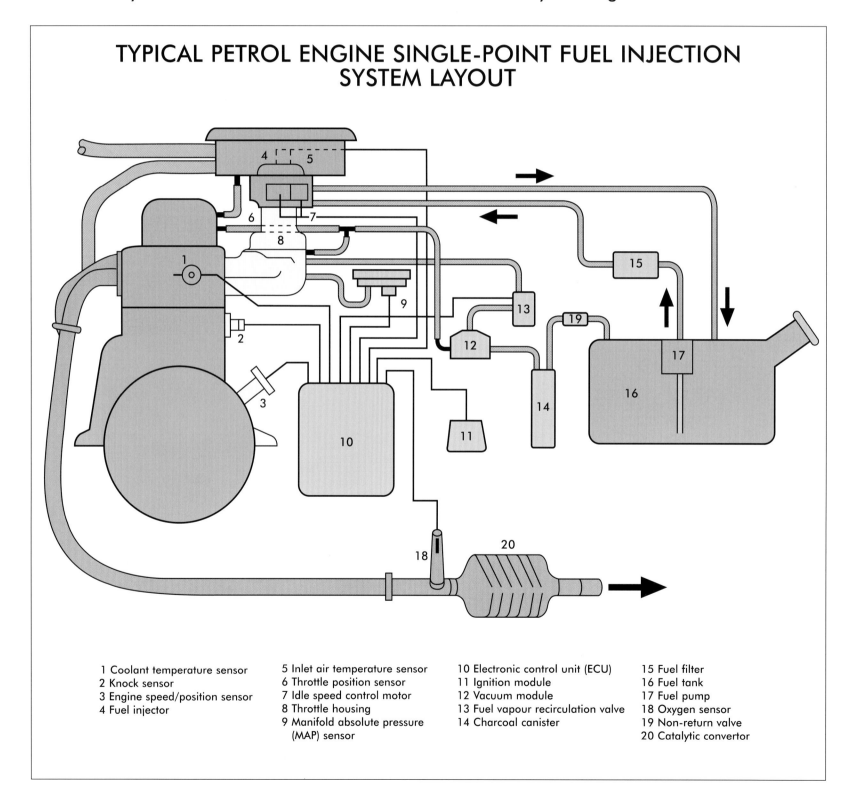

TYPICAL PETROL ENGINE SINGLE-POINT FUEL INJECTION SYSTEM LAYOUT

1 Coolant temperature sensor
2 Knock sensor
3 Engine speed/position sensor
4 Fuel injector
5 Inlet air temperature sensor
6 Throttle position sensor
7 Idle speed control motor
8 Throttle housing
9 Manifold absolute pressure (MAP) sensor
10 Electronic control unit (ECU)
11 Ignition module
12 Vacuum module
13 Fuel vapour recirculation valve
14 Charcoal canister
15 Fuel filter
16 Fuel tank
17 Fuel pump
18 Oxygen sensor
19 Non-return valve
20 Catalytic convertor

Petrol engines

Air passes through the air filter into the inlet manifold, where it is mixed with fuel, before passing through the inlet valves into the engine cylinders.

On older engines, a carburettor is used to mix the fuel and air. A carburettor uses the flow of air to suck fuel into the engine. It doesn't give enough control over the fuel/air mixture to enable an engine to meet modern emissions regulations.

A fuel injection system is much more efficient than a carburettor, and allows fine control of the fuel/air mixture. On a single-point fuel injection system, a fuel injector is used to spray fuel into the inlet manifold, where it is mixed with air before passing to the cylinders. On a multi-point fuel injection system, one fuel injector is used for each cylinder in the engine.

Diesel engines

The air passes through the air filter into the inlet manifold, and into the engine cylinders. A fuel injection pump pumps fuel to a fuel injector for each cylinder.

On an indirect injection diesel engine, the fuel injector pumps the fuel into a swirl chamber mounted in the cylinder head above the cylinder, which swirls the fuel around to mix it with the air in the cylinder. On a direct injection diesel engine, the fuel injector pumps the fuel directly into the cylinder, where it is mixed with the air.

TYPICAL DIESEL ENGINE FUEL SYSTEM LAYOUT

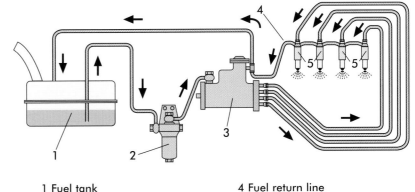

1 Fuel tank
2 Fuel filter
3 Fuel injection pump

4 Fuel return line
5 Fuel injectors
Arrows show direction of fuel flow

What to check

Air filters, fuel filters, and (on petrol engines) the spark plugs, should all be renewed at the recommended intervals. Always make sure that the correct types of filter and spark plugs are used.

Modern fuel and ignition systems are very reliable, and most problems are due to damp, or to poor or dirty electrical connections.

- Always make sure that you have plenty of fuel in the tank – if you run out of fuel, dirt may be drawn into the fuel system from the fuel tank.

- Always renew the components at the manufacturer's recommended intervals – see "Fluids and filters", and "Spark plugs".
- Regularly check all electrical connections and wiring.
- On diesel engines, drain water from the fuel filter regularly – see "Fluids and filters".
- Spray damp electrical connections with water dispersant.
- Regularly check the fuel line connections under the bonnet for leaks – fuel leaks are dangerous as well as expensive.

Spark plugs

Spark plugs are fitted to petrol engines, and their job is to ignite the fuel/air mixture in the cylinders at the correct instant.

When the ignition system sends a voltage down the HT lead to the spark plug, the high voltage causes a spark to jump between the spark plug centre electrode and the earth electrode. The spark ignites the explosive fuel/air mixture which pushes the piston down the cylinder.

The "spark plug gap" (the gap between the earth electrode and the centre electrode) can be adjusted to suit a particular engine. The size of the gap is very important, because it controls the way the fuel/air mixture burns. Some spark plugs have more than one earth electrode.

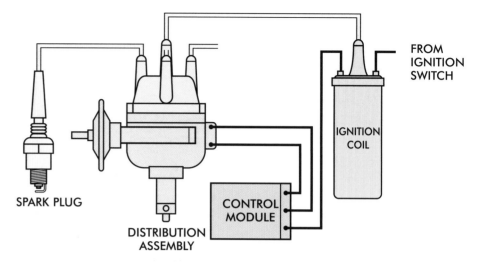

TYPICAL IGNITION SYSTEM LAYOUT

Buying the correct spark plugs

If you fit the wrong plugs, the engine may not run properly, and in the worst case, serious engine damage could be caused. Usually, your car's handbook will tell you which plugs to fit, and each plug manufacturer has an applications guide. You can buy new plugs from an authorised dealer, or from motor factors and car accessory shops. You'll need to know the make and model of your car, the engine size, and year of manufacture. If you're in any doubt as to which plugs to fit, always check your car manufacturer's recommendations.

Glow plugs

Glow plugs are fitted to diesel engines to help start the engine from cold and to reduce smoke immediately after start-up. A diesel engine relies on a high temperature in the cylinder to ignite the fuel/air mixture (see "How does it work") – a cold engine, combined with cold air being drawn into the engine, won't give a high enough temperature.

The glow plugs are electrical heater elements (called glow plugs because they glow red hot!) and usually (though not always), one glow plug is fitted to each cylinder.

On most modern diesel engines, the glow plugs are controlled automatically by an electronic control unit. The glow plugs are switched on when the ignition is switched on, and a warning light on the instrument panel is activated to show that the glow plugs are working.

The usual method used to start a diesel engine is:
a) Turn the ignition key until the glow plug warning light comes on.
b) Wait until the glow plug warning light goes out.
c) Start the engine.

The glow plug warning light goes out when the glow plugs have heated up enough to start the engine – if you turn the key straight to the start position without pausing for the light to go out, the engine may not start, or will start with difficulty and make a lot of smoke.

Glow plugs deteriorate very slowly, so there's no need for regular checking or renewal. However, if you have starting problems or experience bad smoking at start-up, have the glow plugs checked - new glow plugs will usually have to be fitted at some point during the car's life.

How to change spark plugs

You will need a set of new spark plugs, a spark plug spanner or socket, a spark plug adjustment tool and feeler gauges, an old small paintbrush, a tube of anti-seize compound, and a length of rubber or plastic tubing to fit over the end of the spark plugs (about 150 mm long).

Before you start, make sure the engine's cold and the ignition is turned off.

The spark plugs are located at the top of the engine, often at the front or back or, on some engines, at the centre of the engine under a cover. Sometimes, you'll need to unbolt surrounding components for access to the plugs.

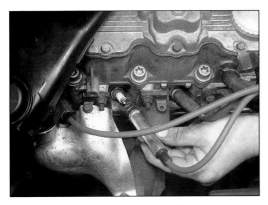

1 Work on one plug at a time, then you won't get the leads muddled up. Gently twist and pull the lead from the top of the first plug – pull on the connector, not on the lead itself.

2 If there's dirt around the top of the plug, brush it away – this will prevent it from falling down into the engine when the plug is removed.

3 Using the spark plug spanner or socket, unscrew and remove the plug.

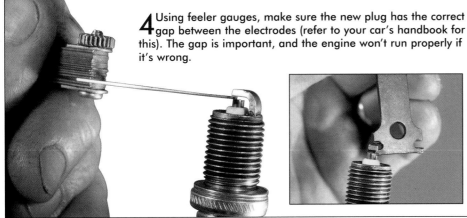

4 Using feeler gauges, make sure the new plug has the correct gap between the electrodes (refer to your car's handbook for this). The gap is important, and the engine won't run properly if it's wrong.

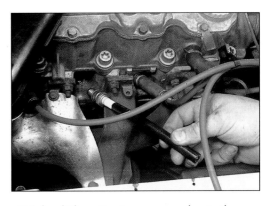

5 Rub a little anti-seize compound onto the threads of the new plug, then use the rubber hose to screw the plug into position. If the threads are crossed, the hose will slip, so you won't damage the threads. If the hose slips, remove the plug, and try again.

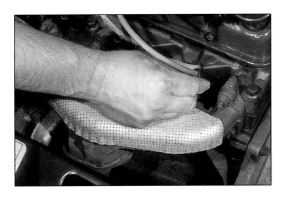

6 Screw the plug in as far as possible using the hose, then tighten it using the spark plug socket. Don't overtighten the plug.

7 Reconnect the lead, then repeat the steps for the other spark plugs in turn.

8 When you've finished, refit any components you had to remove for access.

Engine management systems

A modern engine fitted with an engine management system gives greater reliability, better fuel economy, better performance, and needs less maintenance than a similar older engine without engine management. Bear in mind that many engine management systems have been developed from systems used in motor racing, where nothing's used unless there's a definite benefit.

How do they work?

Various sensors are fitted around the engine. Each sensor produces an electrical signal, and the signal changes as the condition being monitored changes. The electrical signals are sent to an electronic control unit, which contains a microprocessor and a memory. The microprocessor processes all the information from the sensors and, by referring to its memory, can tell exactly what conditions the engine is running under . The control unit is able to "look up" values stored in its memory, and decide how much fuel the engine needs, and what the ignition timing (petrol engines) or injection timing (diesel engines) should be at that particular instant. The control unit also controls the engine idle speed and the emission control systems.

On-board diagnostics

Engine management systems usually have an on-board diagnostic system (or self-diagnostic system) which is used to store details of any faults. If a component is faulty, the system stores a fault code in the control unit. The fault code can be read using a fault code reader, or sometimes a diagnostic light fitted on the car, to indicate which component is faulty. This allows faults to be traced quickly and easily.

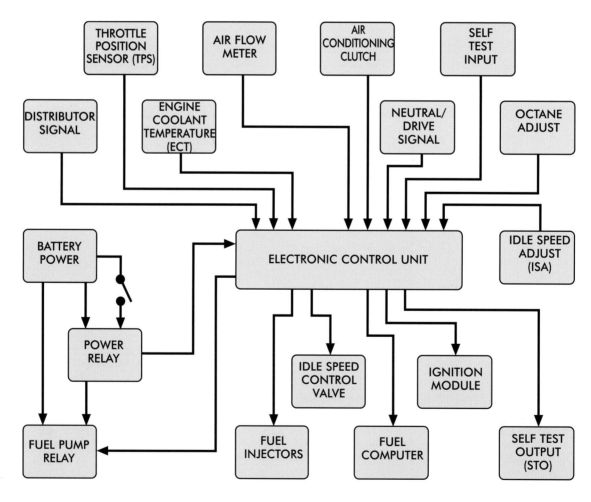

TYPICAL ENGINE MANAGEMENT SYSTEM ELECTRONIC CONTROL UNIT INPUTS AND OUTPUTS

Smoky exhaust

White smoke from the exhaust for a few seconds when you start the car first thing in the morning is no problem – it's just condensation from the exhaust turning into steam. The smoke should stop once the engine starts to warm up. Many diesel engines smoke heavily (black smoke) if you accelerate very hard after driving normally for a long time – again, it's nothing to worry about.

White smoke

Most often caused by coolant getting into the engine's cylinders, maybe from a leaking cylinder head gasket. Often you'll be topping-up the coolant more than usual, and the engine oil level might seem to rise (as coolant leaks into it). This could be serious - have the problem checked out as soon as possible.

Diesel engines make a certain amount of white smoke when starting up, especially in cold weather. If it seems to be excessive, have the glow plugs checked.

On turbocharged engines, white smoke could be due to a leaking oil seal in the turbocharger. Have the problem checked out immediately, as the turbocharger will fail very quickly if the oil is leaking out.

Bluish white smoke

Usually caused by an oil leak inside the engine, this is normally due to worn oil seals inside the cylinder head (not a huge problem), or worn engine bearings or cylinder bores (more serious). You'll often find that you're topping-up the oil more than usual. Have the engine checked before the problem develops into something serious.

Blue smoke on diesels can be caused by a problem with the fuel injection system. Get expert advice before jumping to conclusions.

Black smoke

Normally caused by too much fuel in the fuel/air mixture (if this happens on a car fitted with a catalytic converter, it could damage the catalyst very quickly, so don't drive the car any further than you have to). Black smoke is often accompanied by an increase in fuel consumption, and a black sooty deposit around the inside of the exhaust tailpipe. Have the problem checked out as soon as you can – the first thing to look for is a dirty air cleaner element.

Otherwise, it's often possible to fix things by making adjustments to the fuel system. If the problem goes on for too long, it could cause engine damage.

Catalytic converters

Catalytic converters are used to cut down the amount of harmful exhaust gases released into the atmosphere through the car's exhaust.

A catalyst is a substance which speeds up a chemical change, without being altered itself. The catalytic converter is a steel canister containing a ceramic honeycomb material coated with catalyst. The exhaust gases pass freely over the honeycomb, where the catalyst speeds up the change of the harmful gases into harmless gases and water vapour.

To avoid damaging the catalyst, the engine must be properly tuned, and unleaded petrol must always be used.

On early petrol-engined cars fitted with a catalytic converter, and on all pre-millennium diesel-engined cars, the catalytic converter works independently, and it relies on a well-maintained engine to work. This type of catalytic converter system is called "open-loop".

On most current petrol-engined cars fitted with a catalytic converter, an oxygen (or "Lambda") sensor is fitted to the exhaust system. This is used by the engine management system to control the fuel/air mixture. If the mixture is kept within certain limits, the catalyst can work at its maximum efficiency. The oxygen sensor sends the engine management system details of how much oxygen is in the exhaust gas, and this is used to automatically control the

fuel/air mixture. This type of catalytic converter system is called "closed-loop".

After a number of years, the catalytic converter will have to be renewed, because the catalyst inside will deteriorate with age. This can be expensive because of the precious metals used to make the catalyst.

Catalytic converters have certain side-effects. Firstly, they only work properly once they heat up to an optimum working temperature, and when they're cold, they hardly reduce pollution at all. If you're following a car fitted with a catalytic converter, you might notice a strong "rotten egg" smell when the car accelerates hard, or when it's under a heavy load climbing a hill – this is due to hydrogen sulphide gas. Another side effect is that cars with a catalytic converter tend to produce more water from the exhaust, especially when the engine's cold, or on a short run – this means that the exhaust system tends to rust more quickly.

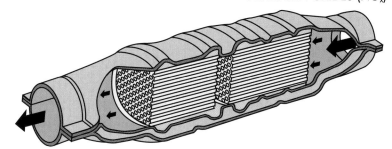

CARBON MONOXIDE (CO)
HYDROCARBONS (HC)
NITROGEN OXIDES (NO_x)

CARBON DIOXIDE (CO_2)
WATER (H_2O)
NITROGEN (N)

CATALYTIC CONVERTER

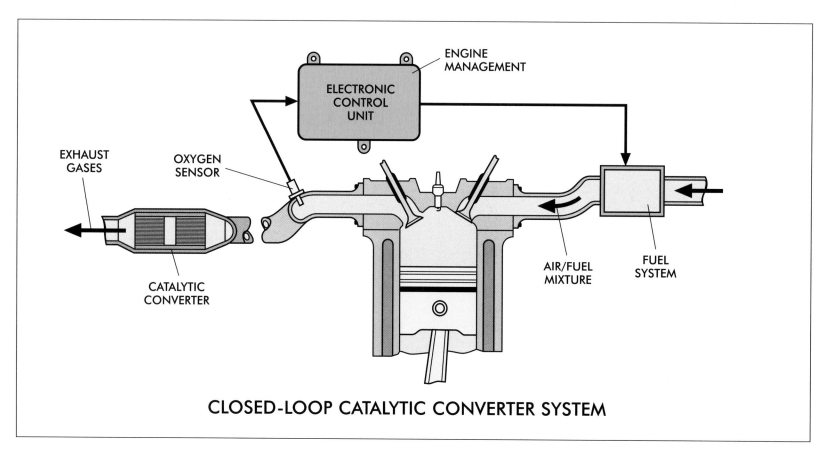

CLOSED-LOOP CATALYTIC CONVERTER SYSTEM

EXHAUST GASES

OXYGEN SENSOR

CATALYTIC CONVERTER

ENGINE MANAGEMENT

ELECTRONIC CONTROL UNIT

AIR/FUEL MIXTURE

FUEL SYSTEM

Cleaning the engine compartment

A little time spent with a rag each time you carry out your routine checks will keep things clean under the bonnet. This will minimise the chances of dirt causing problems, help you spot any fluid leaks in good time, and prevent you getting so dirty in the event of a minor breakdown.

Cleaning for the first time?

You will need a quantity of rag, engine cleaner/degreaser (if the engine is very dirty), access to a working hosepipe, plastic bags and elastic bands.

Before you start, wear old clothes, gloves and eye protection.

You're likely to need more than just rags. The best course of action is to take the car to a garage with steam-cleaning facilities - they'll either do the job for you or advise you on using their equipment.

Some manufacturers apply anti-corrosion wax to the engine compartment which, though it soon looks like caked-on dirt or rust, is intended to be left in place, or renewed after chemical cleaning. Refer to your car's handbook for the maker's recommendations, and where appropriate avoid removing this protective coating.

1 Before starting to clean the engine, cover the coil, distributor and spark plug leads with plastic bags (secured with elastic bands) to prevent chemicals or water getting into them. Cover the back of the alternator and exposed drivebelts and pulleys too. On diesel engines, protect the fuel injection pump.

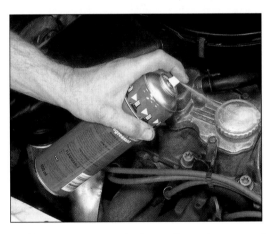

2 You can remove caked-on grime using an engine cleaner spray. Follow the application instructions on the can. Hose off the engine, ensuring the plastic bags stay in place. Let any surplus water drain off, then remove the protective bags carefully to avoid splashing water onto the electrics.

3 It's a good idea to spray vulnerable areas like ignition components with a water dispersant spray - but don't spray drivebelts, brakes or the exhaust! Re-lubricate any moving parts from which oil or grease may have been washed away.

Auxiliary drivebelts

Auxiliary drivebelts are usually driven by a pulley on the end of the crankshaft and drive the engine ancillaries, such as the alternator, power steering and air conditioning compressor and, on some cars, the coolant pump. One drivebelt may drive all the ancillaries, or several separate drivebelts may be used.

On diesel-engined cars, the fuel injection pump may be driven by an auxiliary drivebelt, or by the engine timing belt - in either case, the belt will be enclosed, and normally won't need any regular attention (except for renewal at the recommended intervals). Diesel engines may also have a belt-driven vacuum pump to provide vacuum for the brake servo (see "Brakes").

Drivebelt checking is part of the maintenance schedule on most cars, and you'll almost certainly have to renew the drivebelt(s) at some stage if you keep the car for any length of time.

Buying a spare auxiliary drivebelt

It's always best to carry the correct spare drivebelt for your particular car. You can buy replacement drivebelts from motor factors or car accessory shops, but you may find you have to go to an authorised dealer. To help find the correct new belt, if possible take the old belt along with you. Drivebelts stretch in use, so don't worry if a new belt is a few millimetres shorter than a used one.

Checking an auxiliary drivebelt

1 It can be tricky to reach a drivebelt, and access may be easiest from under the car (you may have to unbolt covers for access). Check the whole length of the belt - you'll probably need to turn the engine. Usually, the easiest way to turn the engine is to use a spanner on the bolt or nut fitted to the pulley end of the crankshaft.

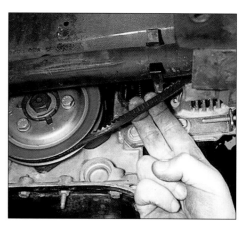

2 Look for cracks, splitting and fraying on the surface of the belt, and check for signs of shiny patches. If you find any damage or wear, a new belt should be fitted.

3 An automatic or a manually-adjustable tensioner may be fitted. A manually-adjustable belt may be adjusted by moving the ancillary it drives (such as the alternator), or there may be a separate adjuster assembly.

4 Most manufacturers specify a tension for each belt, but you should be able to tension a belt correctly by a little trial-and-error. The belt must be tight enough to stop slipping, but not so tight that it strains the ancillaries – if you can push the belt down by about 5 to 10 mm using light finger pressure at the middle of the longest belt run between the pulleys, this should be good enough for most engines.

5 A belt will squeal if it's too slack, especially when pulling away from a standstill. A belt that's too tight may "hum".

Can I drive the car with a broken auxiliary drivebelt?

It's a good idea to carry a spare drivebelt in your car, in case you need it – even if you don't fit it yourself, you'll have the correct belt for someone else to fit for you.

One belt may drive more than one auxiliary, so make sure you know exactly what was driven by the broken drivebelt before you decide whether it's safe to carry on driving!

Broken coolant pump drivebelt	Don't drive the car. If you do, the engine will overheat very quickly.
Broken alternator drivebelt	It's OK to drive on for a short distance. The alternator won't charge the battery, so the alternator warning light will come on and the battery will soon go flat, at which stage the engine will stop.
Broken power steering pump drivebelt	It's OK to drive the car. You'll still be able to steer, but you may need a lot of effort to turn the steering wheel.
Broken air conditioning compressor drivebelt	It's OK to drive the car, but the air conditioning won't work.
Broken fuel injection pump drivebelt (diesel engines)	The engine will stop, so you won't be able to drive the car! Fitting a new injection pump drivebelt isn't a job which can be done at the roadside, so you'll need to call for help.
Broken vacuum pump drivebelt (diesel engines)	It's OK to drive the car. The brakes will still work, but you'll need to push the brake pedal harder than normal to stop the car.
Broken hydraulic pump drivebelt (some middle-sized and all larger Citroëns)	Don't drive the car. The brakes will stop working after a few applications and the suspension will be down on its stops.

Timing belts

A timing belt drives the engine camshaft(s) from the crankshaft – see "How does it work?". The timing belt runs around sprockets on the crankshaft and camshaft(s), and may also drive engine ancillaries.

A tensioner is fitted to keep the belt tight. The tensioner may be automatic, or it could be manually-adjustable.

Timing belts don't last for the lifetime of the car, and **must** be renewed at or before the recommended intervals – if a timing belt breaks when the engine is running, it could cause very serious engine damage.

Renewing the timing belt can be a tricky job, and it's best to have it done by a suitably-equipped garage.

Not all cars have timing belts – some may have a timing chain instead. Often, the engine specifications in your car's handbook will tell you whether the engine has "belt-driven" or "chain-driven" camshaft(s) – if not, contact an authorised dealer or your car manufacturer to find out.

Emissions and emission control

When fuel/air mixture is burnt inside an internal combustion engine, exhaust gases are produced. The exhaust gases pass through the car's exhaust system out into the atmosphere. The gases released into the atmosphere are known as exhaust emissions.

Why do we have emission control?

In recent years, it's been discovered that pollution is having an effect on the earth's atmosphere. Pollution builds up in the atmosphere, and combines to cause problems such as smog, as well as health problems for people living in highly-polluted city areas. It's also believed that pollution, particularly from carbon dioxide, is contributing to the "greenhouse effect", which may be damaging the upper atmosphere, causing changes in weather patterns, and gradual global warming.

The best way to cut down on pollution from cars is to reduce the number of cars on the roads, and some countries are trying to do this by improving public transport, and by increasing taxes on fuel and cars. As there are still huge numbers of cars in use, and the numbers are unlikely to fall significantly in the near future, regulations have been introduced to cut down the amount of pollution produced by car exhausts.

What can I do?

There are ways you can reduce emissions even further.

Do you really need to use your car?

If you only need to travel a short distance, do you really have to take your car? Emissions (and fuel consumption) are at their highest when the engine is cold, and the engine won't warm up properly on a short journey. Could you walk or cycle instead of taking the car, or if you live in a large town or city, could you use public transport?

Driving style

Driving style can have a significant effect on emissions and fuel consumption. Basically, the smoother the driving style, the lower the emissions will be.

Maintenance

A well-maintained car will always produce lower emissions than a similar poorly-maintained example.

What systems are fitted?

All modern engines are designed with low emissions in mind, and using modern engine management systems helps to reduce emissions by giving much better control of the engine. This means that the engine burns the fuel/air mixture more efficiently, to produce less pollution.

Emission control systems are fitted to reduce emissions further, in order to meet the strict regulations in force in most countries.

Catalytic converter

An explanation of catalytic converters is given earlier in this Chapter.

Exhaust gas recirculation (EGR)

This system diverts some of the exhaust gas from the exhaust system back into the engine. The recirculated exhaust gas is then drawn into the cylinders with fresh fuel/air mixture, and burnt. The effect of this is to reduce the amount of unburnt fuel passing into the exhaust system. The amount of exhaust gas drawn into the engine is controlled by a valve, which makes sure that the recirculated gas and the fresh fuel/air mixture is burnt as efficiently as possible.

Fuel evaporative control system (EVAP)

This system is only used on petrol engines. It collects fuel vapour from the fuel tank when the engine is stopped, instead of releasing it into the atmosphere. The fuel vapour is stored in a charcoal canister (the charcoal absorbs the fuel vapour). When the engine is running, the vapour is drawn into the engine and burnt. The amount of vapour drawn into the engine is usually controlled by a valve, which makes sure that the vapour and the fresh fuel/air mixture is burnt as efficiently as possible. As the vapour is drawn from the canister, fresh air is fed in, effectively cleaning the charcoal.

Pulse air system

This system is becoming less common because of the improvement in the control and efficiency of modern catalytic converters. Fresh air is introduced into the exhaust manifold through tubes, and this increases the temperature of the exhaust gases. This in turn causes the catalyst to warm up more quickly.

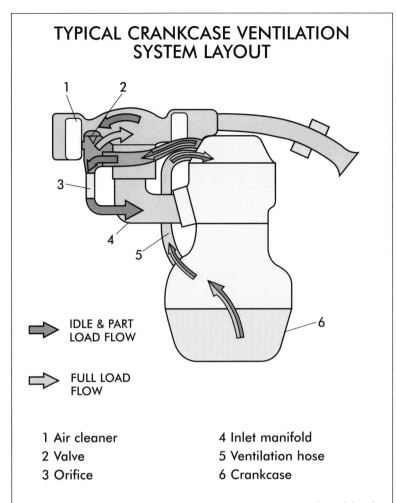

TYPICAL CRANKCASE VENTILATION SYSTEM LAYOUT

→ IDLE & PART LOAD FLOW

→ FULL LOAD FLOW

1 Air cleaner
2 Valve
3 Orifice
4 Inlet manifold
5 Ventilation hose
6 Crankcase

Oil fumes from the engine's crankcase are recirculated back into the engine, instead of being released directly into the atmosphere. The fumes are drawn into the cylinders with fresh air/fuel mixture and burnt.

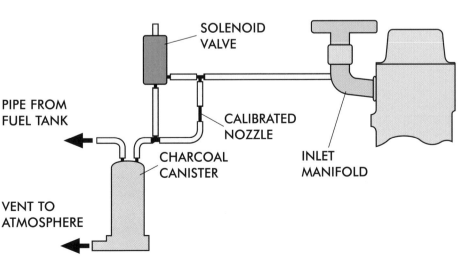

TYPICAL FUEL EVAPORATIVE CONTROL SYSTEM (EVAP) LAYOUT

Cooling and heating

The cooling system is vital, because it stops the engine overheating. It also keeps the engine at an efficient working temperature, and provides heat for the car interior heater. The cooling system consists of a radiator, a coolant (water) pump, a cooling fan, a thermostat, and an expansion tank.

The heating system is really part of the engine cooling system, and consists of a heater matrix, a blower motor, a control panel, and various flaps and air ducts inside the car.

Keeping the engine cool

On all modern cars, the cooling system is pressurised, and consists of a radiator (mounted at the front of the engine compartment), a coolant (water) pump (mounted on the engine), a cooling fan (which cools the radiator), a thermostat, and an expansion tank.

The radiator usually has two narrow tanks, joined by a honeycombed metal matrix (sometimes called a core). The coolant (a mixture of water and antifreeze) flows from one tank, through the matrix to the other tank. On some cars with automatic transmission, a transmission fluid cooler is built into the radiator. The radiator relies on the flow of air through the matrix produced by the car's forward motion, supplemented by the cooling fan when necessary, to cool the coolant inside.

The coolant pump is driven by the engine's timing belt, or by an auxiliary drivebelt – see "The engine". Most coolant pumps consist of a rotating impeller inside a housing.

The cooling fan draws cool air over the radiator when the speed of the car is too low, or the air temperature is too high, to give enough cooling. The cooling fan is usually electrically-operated, although some older cars may have a belt-driven fan. A few cars have a viscous fan

attached to one of the engine pulleys – a viscous fluid coupling causes the fan to turn as the engine heats up.

The thermostat is normally fitted inside a housing on the engine. Its job is to allow the engine to warm up quickly by restricting the flow of coolant to the radiator when cold, and also to regulate the normal operating temperature of the engine.

A pressure cap is fitted to the system, either in the expansion tank or in the radiator. The pressure cap effectively pressurises the cooling system as the temperature rises, which raises the boiling point of the coolant. It acts as a safety valve by venting steam or hot coolant if the pressure rises above a certain level. The pressure cap also acts as a vacuum relief valve to stop a vacuum forming in the system as it cools.

The expansion tank allows room for the coolant to expand as it heats up. Any air or gas bubbles which form in the coolant return to the expansion tank, and are released in the air space above the coolant.

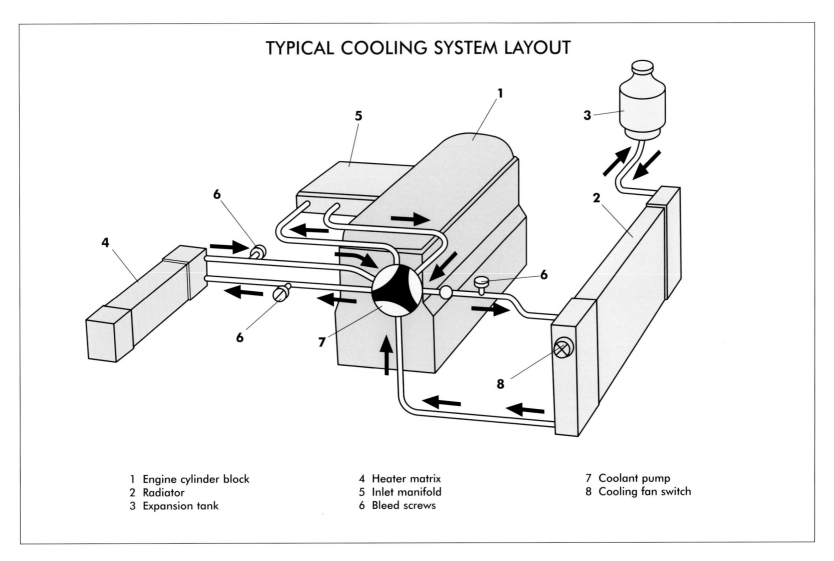

TYPICAL COOLING SYSTEM LAYOUT

1 Engine cylinder block	4 Heater matrix	7 Coolant pump
2 Radiator	5 Inlet manifold	8 Cooling fan switch
3 Expansion tank	6 Bleed screws	

Overheating

Overheating is a serious problem, and can be caused by a number of things. If you're driving on a hot day in summer, your car will overheat much more easily in traffic than on a cold winter's day, but provided your car's been properly maintained, you shouldn't really have any problems.

When the engine gets hot, the cooling fan should cut in to lower the temperature. Normally you'll be able to see this on the temperature gauge – the temperature will go up until the cooling fan cuts in, then the temperature will fall. The cycle might repeat several times until you start moving forwards fast enough for the airflow to cool the radiator without needing the fan.

If the temperature gauge stays in the red, don't be tempted to carry on driving – stop as soon as possible. (As an emergency measure, turning the heater blower onto full speed and selecting maximum heat will bring the temperature down a little, at the cost of some discomfort to the occupants.)

Temperature gauge faulty?

If you can't find any obvious signs of overheating (steam, banging noises, hot smells), are you sure your temperature gauge is working properly? If the fuel gauge has also been erratic, or if (for instance) switching the lights on or off causes an immediate jump in temperature, suspect the gauge. A garage or auto electrical specialist will be able to test it for you.

Is the thermostat faulty?

The thermostat controls the coolant flow. When the engine's cold, the thermostat is shut, which allows the engine to warm up quickly. As the engine warms up, the thermostat opens, allowing coolant to flow through the radiator, and preventing the engine from getting too hot.

If a thermostat sticks closed, it will cause overheating, and if it sticks open, the engine will tend to run cooler than normal.

To check for a thermostat which is stuck closed, take the car for a short run (about 10 minutes should be enough), then stop the car, open the bonnet and put your hand on the radiator top hose (take care, the hose and surrounding components may be very hot!). You should be able to feel hot coolant passing through the hose – if not, the thermostat is probably stuck closed, and there is a high chance that your engine will overheat.

To check for a thermostat which is stuck open, start the engine, and run it for about 10 minutes, then switch on the car's heater, turn the temperature control to the maximum position, and check for warm air. If the air is cool, or only luke-warm, the thermostat is probably stuck open.

If you think your car might have a faulty thermostat, take it to a garage for a check – fitting a new thermostat is usually a straightforward job, and shouldn't be too expensive. If your car is a few years old, it's a good idea to have the thermostat changed every couple of years (at the same time as you change the coolant) as a precaution against any problems.

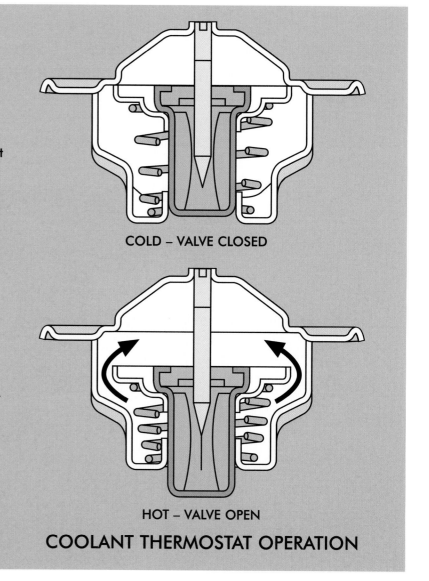

COLD – VALVE CLOSED

HOT – VALVE OPEN

COOLANT THERMOSTAT OPERATION

Is the radiator blocked?

Suspect a blockage of some kind if the fan is working, the coolant level and the thermostat are OK but the engine still overheats. An external blockage is usually caused by a build-up of dead insects and dirt between the fins of the radiator matrix so the radiator can't do its job properly. Use an old paint brush to free debris from the radiator fins.

It's rare for a radiator to get blocked internally unless servicing has been neglected. (Note that a few manufacturers use "lifetime" coolant, which is designed to last the life of the car – check in your car's handbook for details.) If you think that the radiator may be blocked, you can buy special flushing compounds which must be used as directed. Alternatively, a garage will be able to drain, clean and refill the cooling system for you. In really bad cases a new radiator will be needed.

Is the coolant level low?

If the coolant level is low, this can cause overheating. Check the coolant level regularly, as described in "Fluids and filters". If the coolant level is low, is it because there's a leak? Refer to "Coolant leaks" for further details.

Is the fan faulty?

The cooling fan on most modern cars is electrically-operated, and is switched on automatically when it's needed. Electric cooling fans are usually operated by a heat-sensitive electric switch located in the coolant circuit. The switch completes the electrical circuit to switch on the fan at a pre-determined temperature. If your car overheats in traffic, but doesn't on the open road, this is a sign that the fan is not operating as it should.

To test the cooling fan, start and run the engine until it reaches normal operating temperature, then continue to run the engine with the car stationary. As the temperature goes up, the cooling fan should cut-in to bring the temperature back to normal. If the cooling fan doesn't switch on, there's a fault with the switch or the fan itself. Take the car to a garage to have the fan and switch checked.

Has the coolant pump failed?

Although it's rare for a coolant pump to fail, if it does happen, the engine will overheat very quickly because no coolant is being pumped round. A failed coolant pump will usually be obvious because it will cause a serious coolant leak from the engine. Often, there will be tell-tale signs of leakage before the pump fails completely.

It's not always the pump itself which fails, it may be just the sealing (a gasket or special sealant) between the pump and the engine. If the pump is driven by an auxiliary drivebelt (see "The engine"), it's possible that the drivebelt is slack (this usually causes a squealing noise), or even that the belt has broken. If the coolant pump is driven by the engine timing belt (see "The engine"), and the timing belt fails, the engine will stop long before it overheats!

If you think that the coolant pump may have failed or its drivebelt has broken, call for help – don't try to drive the car.

. . . or are you just overworking your car?

If overheating is only a problem when you're towing a caravan over an Alpine pass, or driving at sustained high speeds in unusually hot weather, it may just be that you're asking too much of your car. Towing in particular makes heavy demands on the engine, cooling system and transmission, and it may be desirable to fit an additional or uprated cooling fan. Ask your garage or a towing specialist if in doubt.

Coolant leaks

Cooling system leaks can be a serious problem because they can cause engine overheating very quickly. Refer to "Troubleshooting" for details of how to identify leaks.

Head gasket

The head gasket seals the engine cylinder head to the cylinder block – see "The engine". Leaks can be a serious problem. Tell-tale signs of a head gasket leak are:

- Coolant in the engine oil – you'll notice a foamy layer on top of the oil when you check the level on the dipstick. You might also find that the oil level seems to rise!
- Engine oil in the coolant – the coolant in the expansion tank will be discoloured, and there may be mayonnaise-like deposits on the sides of the tank, and on the top surface of the coolant.
- Overheating – keep an eye on the temperature gauge.
- A steady stream of bubbles in the coolant when the engine is running.
- Loss of power – the engine will almost certainly be down on power.
- Whistling or wheezing noises – if there's a very bad leak, you may notice noises, especially when the engine is under load.

A leaking head gasket is a serious problem, and you should take your car to a garage to have the problem fixed before it gets any worse.

Coolant pump

Leaks can usually be spotted from the traces of coolant running down the engine near the pump.

It might be possible to fix the leak by having a new gasket fitted or by re-sealing the pump. Sometimes, the pump internal seals can fail, in which case you'll have to have a new pump fitted.

Coolant hoses

Rubber coolant hoses deteriorate with age, and eventually they can crack or perish. To check a hose (wait until the engine has cooled down – hot coolant can cause scalding!), squeeze and stretch it between your fingers – this will tend to open out any cracks or splits.

Radiator

Radiators tend to deteriorate with age, and they're easily damaged.

You should be able to see traces of a leak on a radiator – look for leaking coolant, or any obvious deposits.

If you think the radiator's leaking, have it checked by a garage or a radiator specialist as soon as possible. You may be able to have the radiator repaired, or you may need a new one.

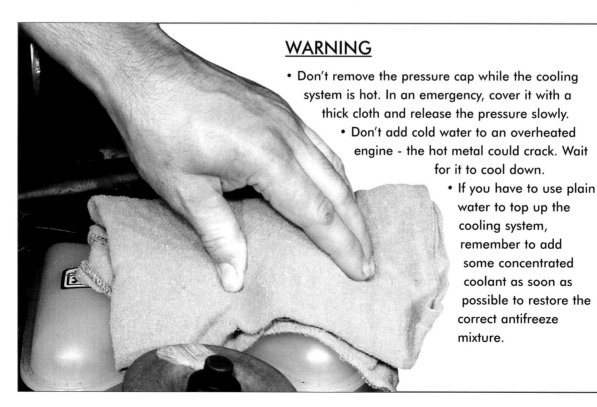

WARNING

- Don't remove the pressure cap while the cooling system is hot. In an emergency, cover it with a thick cloth and release the pressure slowly.
- Don't add cold water to an overheated engine - the hot metal could crack. Wait for it to cool down.
- If you have to use plain water to top up the cooling system, remember to add some concentrated coolant as soon as possible to restore the correct antifreeze mixture.

Faulty pressure cap?

A faulty pressure cap will effectively lower the boiling point of the coolant, which means that coolant will be lost through boiling.

A garage will be able to test the pressure cap for you – if it's faulty, have it renewed.

Keeping the interior comfortable

A standard car heating system is really part of the engine cooling system, and consists of a heater matrix (very similar to the cooling system radiator), a blower motor, a control panel, and various flaps and air ducts inside the car.

Coolant flows through the heater matrix. Cool air passes into the ventilation ducting through grilles, usually at the front of the car below the windscreen. Some of the air is directed through the heater matrix fins, picking up heat. The positions of the various flaps alter the mixture of hot and cold air, and direct the airflow to different parts of the interior. The heater controls may be connected to the flaps by levers or cables, or sometimes vacuum or electric motors may be used to move the flaps. The airflow can be increased by switching on the blower motor, which forces air through the ducts.

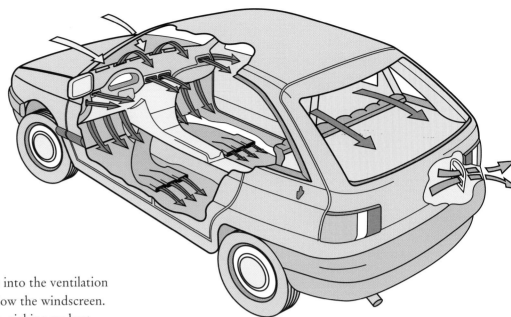

TYPICAL HEATING/VENTILATION SYSTEM AIRFLOW

It's too hot or cold!

If adjusting the heater controls doesn't seem to make any difference, the most likely cause is a badly adjusted or broken heater control. A garage will be able to check the heater controls for you.

Falling leaves and dead insects can collect in the intake grilles and block them, and sometimes debris can pass into the ducts – you may notice an annoying rustling noise (dead leaves) when you turn the heater blower on. You'll usually be able to see if the intake grilles are blocked: the intake grilles are usually at the back of the engine compartment, below the windscreen. If debris has found its way into the ducting, try turning the heater blower motor control to the maximum position, and move the other heater controls to move the control flaps back-and-forth – hopefully, this will dislodge the debris, and you'll be able to pick it out through the heating/ventilation nozzles in the facia.

If it's still too hot or cold, it's possible that the cooling system thermostat is faulty (see "Is the thermostat faulty?").

I can smell antifreeze

If you can smell antifreeze (a sweet, sickly smell) inside the car, the most likely cause is a leaking heater matrix.

Often, the heater matrix is mounted behind the facia so check the carpets under the facia to see if they're damp. If they are, then the matrix is almost certainly leaking. If the leak is very serious, you may also notice a drop in the coolant level.

Sometimes you may find that a smell of antifreeze is due to a leak under the bonnet – in either case have the problem checked out by a garage as soon as possible. Any sort of coolant leak can eventually cause the engine to overheat (see "Overheating").

The transmission

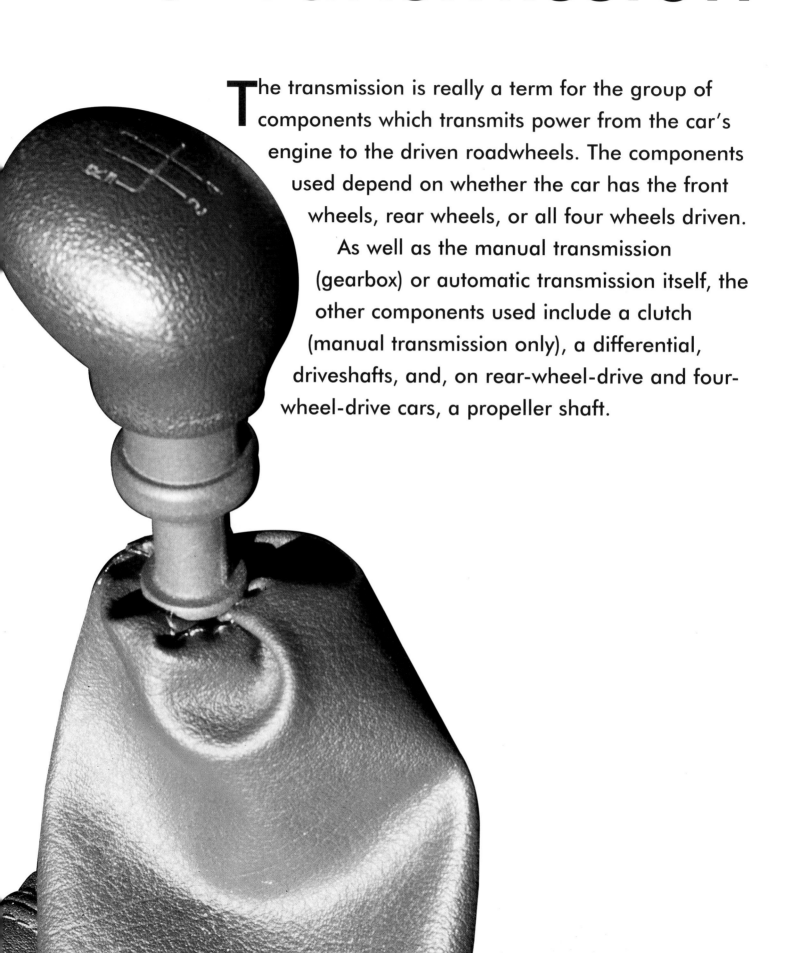

The transmission is really a term for the group of components which transmits power from the car's engine to the driven roadwheels. The components used depend on whether the car has the front wheels, rear wheels, or all four wheels driven. As well as the manual transmission (gearbox) or automatic transmission itself, the other components used include a clutch (manual transmission only), a differential, driveshafts, and, on rear-wheel-drive and four-wheel-drive cars, a propeller shaft.

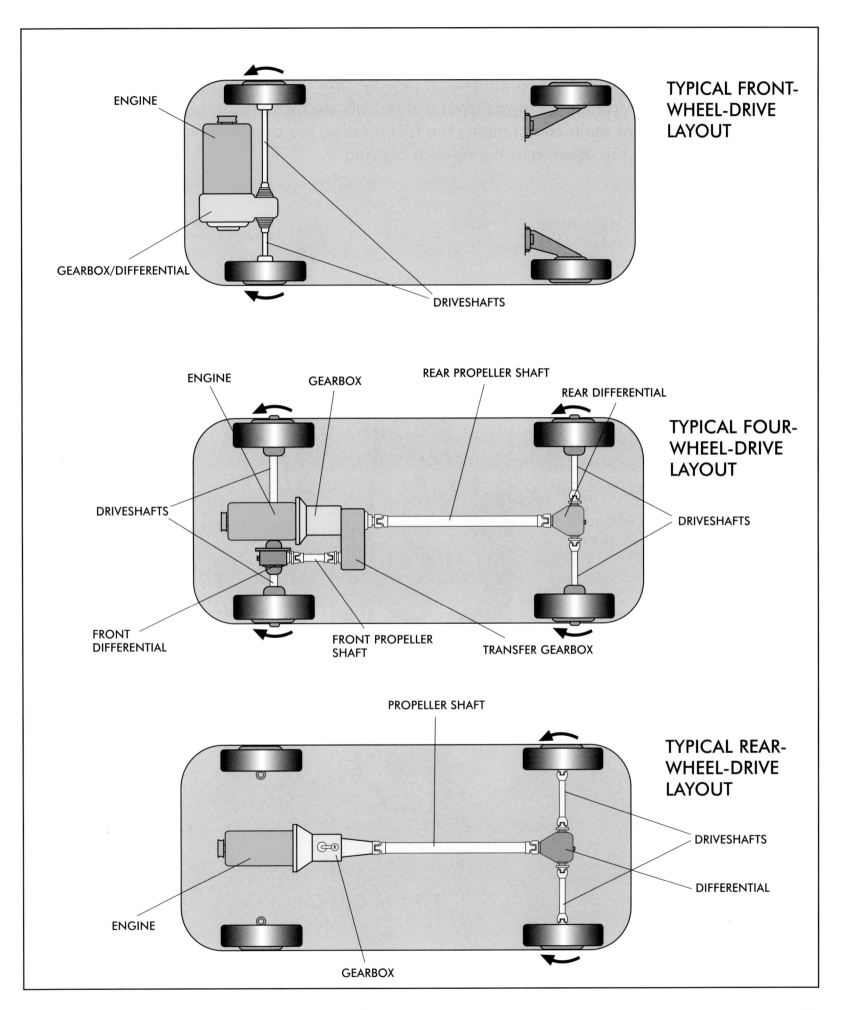

ENGINE

GEARBOX/DIFFERENTIAL

DRIVESHAFTS

TYPICAL FRONT-WHEEL-DRIVE LAYOUT

ENGINE

GEARBOX

REAR PROPELLER SHAFT

REAR DIFFERENTIAL

DRIVESHAFTS

DRIVESHAFTS

FRONT DIFFERENTIAL

FRONT PROPELLER SHAFT

TRANSFER GEARBOX

TYPICAL FOUR-WHEEL-DRIVE LAYOUT

PROPELLER SHAFT

DRIVESHAFTS

DIFFERENTIAL

ENGINE

GEARBOX

TYPICAL REAR-WHEEL-DRIVE LAYOUT

Clutch

The clutch's job is to allow a smooth transfer of power from the engine to the transmission when moving the car away from a standstill, and when changing gear. The clutch has five main components; the friction disc, the pressure plate, the diaphragm spring, the cover, and the release bearing.

The friction disc is free to slide along the splines of the gearbox input shaft, and is held in place between the engine flywheel and the clutch pressure plate by the diaphragm spring pushing against the pressure plate. Friction material is riveted to both sides of the friction disc. Spring cushioning between the friction material and the centre of the friction disc absorbs transmission shocks, and helps to give a smooth take-up of power as the clutch is engaged.

The diaphragm spring is mounted on pins in the cover, and is held in place by thin metal fulcrum rings built into the cover.

The release bearing is fitted on a guide sleeve at the front of the gearbox, and the bearing is free to slide on the sleeve, under the action of the release arm, which pivots inside the end of the gearbox casing.

The release arm is operated by the clutch cable, or on some cars by a hydraulic system.

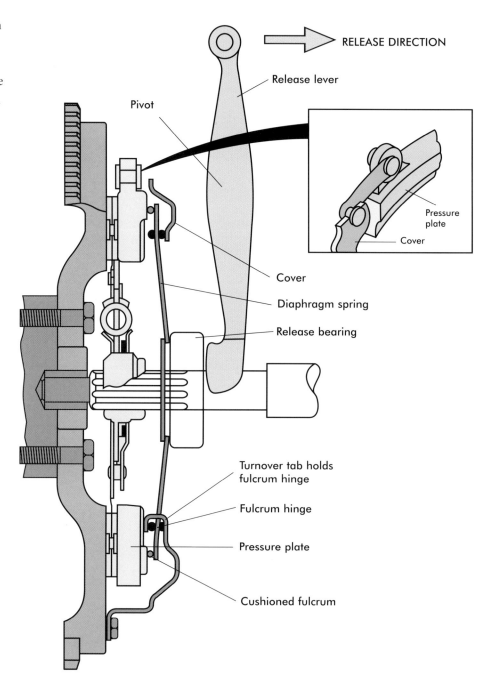

RELEASE DIRECTION

Pivot

Release lever

Pressure plate

Cover

Cover

Diaphragm spring

Release bearing

Turnover tab holds fulcrum hinge

Fulcrum hinge

Pressure plate

Cushioned fulcrum

TYPICAL CLUTCH COMPONENT LAYOUT

How to look after your clutch

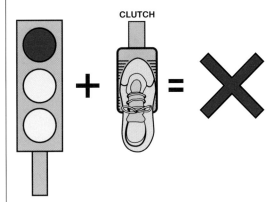

Eventually, the friction material on the friction disc will wear away. When this happens, the clutch will probably start to slip. The life of the clutch depends on the type of car, the type of clutch and, most importantly, the driving style and conditions.

Do's and don'ts

Do . . .
– operate the clutch quickly and smoothly – slipping the clutch causes unnecessary wear.
– make sure that the clutch is correctly adjusted, if you have an adjustable clutch.
– check the fluid level at the recommended intervals if you have a hydraulic clutch.

Don't . . .
– sit with the car in gear and your foot on the clutch at traffic lights and busy junctions.
– rest your foot on the clutch pedal – this will cause premature wear.
– slip the clutch to stop the car from rolling back when carrying out an uphill start.
– rev the engine as you change gear – this will cause increased wear.
– just suddenly take your foot off the clutch when moving away from rest – always release the clutch smoothly and gradually.

Is my clutch worn out?

There are two main symptoms which can indicate worn or contaminated clutch components – clutch slip, and clutch judder. A slipping clutch will be slow to take up drive, and the engine revs will rise without the car's speed increasing, especially when moving off or going up hills. Clutch judder is a jerking, shuddering or shaking which happens as the clutch is engaged, or during acceleration.

If the clutch is contaminated, it may not be worn, but the friction disc will still probably have to be renewed.

Here are a few possible causes of clutch judder:

• Worn clutch friction disc or pressure plate.
• Contaminated clutch – the contamination could be caused by oil from a leaking engine oil seal, a leaking transmission oil seal, or hydraulic fluid from a leaking hydraulic clutch cylinder.
• A loose or broken engine or transmission mounting, or loose engine-to-transmission bolts.
• Worn transmission components.

If you think that the clutch seems to have worn out prematurely, here are a few possible causes:

• A badly adjusted, faulty or sticking clutch release mechanism.
• Loose clutch securing bolts.
• Weak clutch pressure plate springs.
• Worn gearbox input shaft.

Before deciding that your clutch is worn out, have the adjustment checked. If you do need to have a new clutch fitted, you'll need to take the car to your local garage, or to a clutch fitting specialist.

Manual transmission (gearbox)

The job of the manual transmission is to allow the driver to select the correct gear to suit the car's speed and the road conditions.

On front-wheel-drive cars, the gearbox usually has two shafts, the input shaft and the output shaft (sometimes called the mainshaft). The shafts run in parallel, next to each other, and the gears on the two shafts are in constant mesh. The gears on the input shaft are permanently fixed to the shaft, but the gears on the output shaft are free to turn (so the output shaft can turn whilst the gears on it stay still).

When a gear is selected, a lever moves a sliding synchromesh hub along the output shaft, which locks the appropriate gear to the shaft. One synchromesh assembly is fitted for each gear. The job of each synchromesh assembly is to allow smooth, quiet gear engagement by making sure that the gear is spinning at the same speed as the output shaft when the two are locked together. Drive is transmitted from the output shaft, by a pinion gear, to the differential (see "Differential"), which is built into the gearbox casing.

On rear-wheel-drive cars, the gearbox usually has three shafts: the input shaft, the output shaft, and a layshaft. The input shaft runs in line with the output shaft, and both the input and output shaft gears are in constant mesh with the layshaft gears. The gears on the input and output shafts are permanently fixed to the shaft, but the gears on the layshaft are free to turn (so the layshaft can turn whilst the gears stay still). When a gear is selected, a lever moves a synchromesh hub along the layshaft, which locks the appropriate gear to the shaft. Drive is transmitted from the output shaft to a propeller shaft, which transmits drive to the rear differential.

Various types of gearbox are used on four-wheel-drive cars, but the most common type is similar to the rear-wheel-drive type described previously.

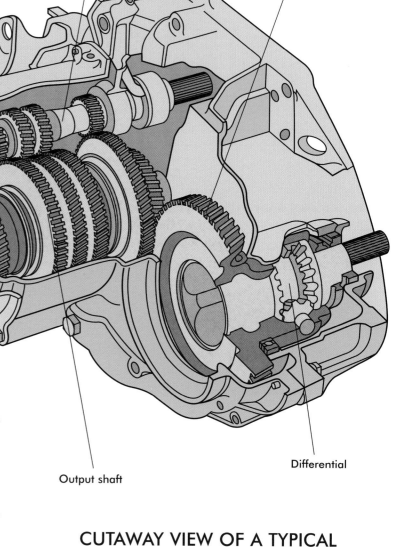

Input shaft

Crown wheel

Differential

Output shaft

CUTAWAY VIEW OF A TYPICAL MANUAL GEARBOX

Selecting the correct gear

Normal driving

If you're driving a car with manual transmission you need to match the gear to the engine speed. The engine will only deliver power smoothly over a relatively small speed range – typically from 1500 to 5000 rpm. At lower speeds it will labour or stall; at higher speeds it will be noisy, thirsty and could be damaged. If the engine's labouring (low revs), you need to change to a lower gear, and if you're running out of acceleration (because the revs are too high), you need to change to a higher gear. Once you get familiar with the car, you'll know which gear you need.

Driving in slippery conditions

If you're driving on a slippery road surface, particularly in winter, using a higher gear (and less engine revs) than normal will give you more traction - try using second gear instead of first when moving away. This is because a higher gear will transmit less power and torque (torque is the pushing force of the wheels on the road surface) to the driven wheels, so they'll be less likely to slip.

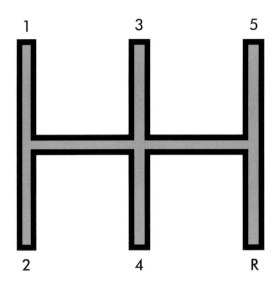

Why is it sometimes tricky to engage reverse gear?

In a manual transmission, the forward gears have synchromesh (see opposite) to help give smooth gear changes. A worn or faulty clutch, or worn synchromesh components can cause noisy gear changes.

Synchromesh isn't normally fitted to reverse gear, so sometimes it can be tricky to get reverse (and it may "crunch" when you do). If you have trouble selecting reverse, here are a couple of tips:

1. Push the clutch pedal down, then pause for a few seconds before selecting reverse. When you push the clutch pedal, the clutch friction disc keeps spinning for a few seconds, along with the gears in the transmission - if you pause, the gears will slow down, and they'll engage more easily.

2. If you still have problems, try moving the gear lever into neutral and release the clutch pedal, then push the clutch pedal down again, and repeat the selection procedure.

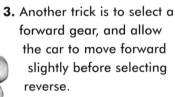

3. Another trick is to select a forward gear, and allow the car to move forward slightly before selecting reverse.

Do's and Don'ts

Do . . .

– match the gear to the engine speed.

– pause for a fraction of a second in neutral before selecting the next gear, to allow time for the synchromesh units to work.

– have the transmission oil level checked at the specified intervals.

Don't . . .

– try to change to a lower gear too early - you could over-rev the engine which can cause serious damage.

– try to change to a higher gear too early - the engine will labour and may stall.

– rest your hand on the gear lever - this puts stress on the transmission components and causes unnecessary wear.

Automatic transmission

There are two basic types of conventional automatic transmission, using a torque converter and a gearbox, or Continuously Variable Transmission (CVT). With either type, gear changing during normal driving is automatic.

In a conventional automatic transmission, the torque converter acts as a fluid coupling between the engine and transmission, taking the place of the clutch in a manual transmission. The torque converter transmits the drive to an "epicyclic" geartrain, which provides several forward gears and reverse gear, depending on which components of the geartrain are held stationary or allowed to turn. The geartrain components are held stationary or released by hydraulic brakes and clutches. A fluid pump built into the transmission provides the hydraulic pressure, via a control unit, to operate the brakes and clutches.

An output shaft transmits power to the differential (front-wheel-drive) or the propeller shaft (rear-wheel-drive).

Continuously variable transmission (CVT)

Several different types of CVT have been produced, but they all work in a similar way. The input shaft drives a cone-shaped pulley, which in turn drives a belt (usually made of metal). The belt drives a second cone-shaped pulley, which is linked to the output shaft. The continuous variation in ratio is produced by allowing the belt to run on a different part of the two pulleys – this is done by a hydraulic control system which moves one half of each pulley towards or away from its remaining half. Drive is transmitted from the output shaft, by a pinion gear, to the differential (see "Differential"), which is built into the gearbox casing.

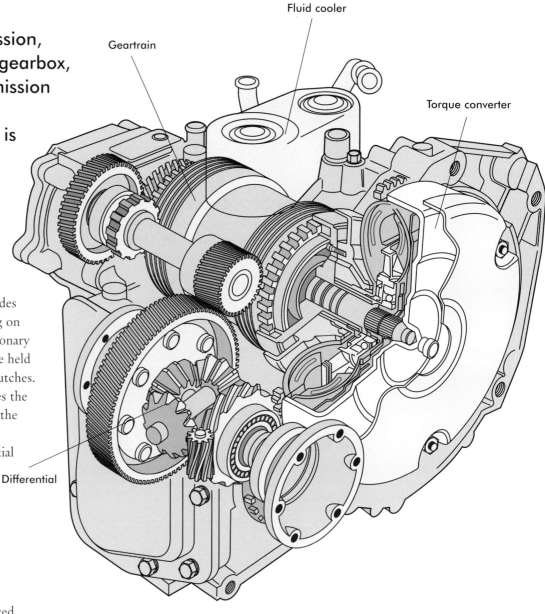

Fluid cooler

Geartrain

Torque converter

Differential

CUTAWAY VIEW OF A TYPICAL CONVENTIONAL AUTOMATIC TRANSMISSION

P

R

N

D

3

2

1

Selecting the correct gear

Normal driving

Select "D" (for Drive). The transmission will change up or down as required. On a conventional automatic you can hear or feel the gear changes taking place; on a CVT all you will notice is a gradual change in the engine note. Some transmissions may have a "Sport" button which allows the transmission to change up at higher engine speeds for sporty driving.

Kickdown

If you press the accelerator to the floor, the transmission will change up at higher engine speeds than if you only press lightly. This gives you better acceleration, but at the expense of increased fuel consumption.

Driving in slippery conditions

If you're driving on a slippery road surface or descending a steep hill, select gears manually (use "2" when moving away from a standstill) – check your car's handbook for details.

Checking the fluid level

Automatic transmissions are complicated, and expensive to repair. As well as lubricating the transmission, the transmission fluid helps to transmit drive from the engine, and keeps the transmission cool. It's very important to check the fluid level regularly (see "Fluids and filters"). If the fluid level gets low, it can rapidly cause problems and expensive damage. Too high a fluid level (as a result of over-enthusiastic topping-up) can also cause damage.

Are automatics thirstier?

Until a few years ago, cars with automatic transmission were slower and used more fuel than their manual transmission counterparts. Modern designs have all but eliminated these problems.

Do's and Don'ts

Do . . .

- check the fluid level regularly, and at the first sign of any problem.
- keep your foot on the brake when stationary unless "P" or "N" is selected.
- select "P" when parking.
- stop completely before selecting "P" or "R".

Don't . . .

- drive the car if the fluid level is low.
- overfill the transmission with fluid – this can cause damage.
- rev the engine when selecting a gear.

Driveshafts

The driveshafts transmit drive from the differential to the wheels. Each driveshaft is fixed to the differential at one end, and to the wheel hub at the other.

On rear-wheel-drive cars with a rigid rear axle assembly, the driveshafts are enclosed and normally run straight from the differential to the wheel hubs, so a straight shaft is all that's required for each driveshaft.

On rear-wheel-drive cars with independent rear suspension, the angle of the driveshafts will change as the suspension moves, so universal joints are incorporated at the ends of the driveshafts to allow for the movement. Modern universal joints don't need any lubrication, so they're maintenance-free.

On front-wheel-drive cars, the angle of the driveshafts will change as the suspension moves, and the angle of the wheels changes as the steering is turned. To allow for the suspension and steering movement, constant velocity joints are incorporated at the ends of the driveshafts. The joints are packed with a special grease, and are covered by flexible rubber gaiters (see "Looking after driveshafts").

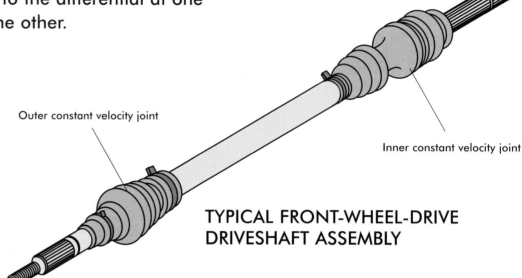

Outer constant velocity joint

Inner constant velocity joint

TYPICAL FRONT-WHEEL-DRIVE DRIVESHAFT ASSEMBLY

Looking after driveshafts

With the exception of a few older rear-wheel-drive cars (which need to have the propeller shaft and/or driveshaft universal joints greased regularly), the driveshafts don't require any routine maintenance.

The driveshafts are under a lot of stress during normal driving, so here are a few tips which will help you to avoid problems.
• On front-wheel-drive cars, the driveshaft rubber gaiters need to be inspected regularly for damage.
• Avoid "racing" starts.
• Avoid accelerating hard with the steering on full-lock.

Propeller shaft

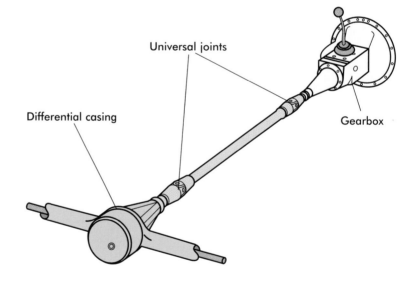

Universal joints

Differential casing

Gearbox

A propeller shaft is used to transmit drive from the transmission to the differential on rear-wheel-drive cars and, depending on the design, from the transfer box to the front and/or rear differentials on four-wheel-drive cars.

Most propeller shafts have at least one universal joint to allow for suspension movement, and the movement of the transmission. Sometimes a bearing is used part way along the propeller shaft to provide extra support.

Differential

When a car's cornering, the wheels on the outside of the turn must travel further than the wheels on the inside. This means that the tyres will tend to resist the car turning. To overcome this problem, a differential is used to allow the wheels to rotate at different rates.

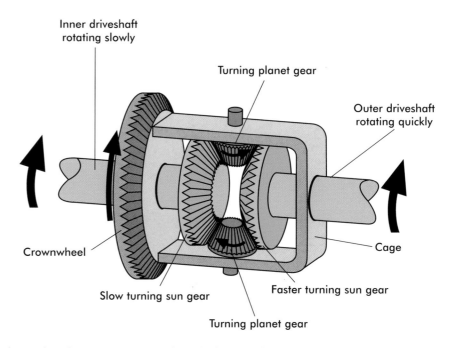

Inner driveshaft rotating slowly

Turning planet gear

Outer driveshaft rotating quickly

Crownwheel

Cage

Slow turning sun gear

Faster turning sun gear

Turning planet gear

The differential consists of a crownwheel, a cage, a cross-shaft, two sun gears, and two planet gears. The cage is bolted to the crownwheel, and supports the sun gears and planet gears. The two planet gears are free to turn on a single cross-shaft, which is fixed across the middle of the cage. Each of the sun gears is attached to one of the driveshafts, and is also in constant mesh with the two planet gears.

When the car moves in a straight line, the crownwheel transmits the drive through the cage, to the cross-shaft. The planet gears are attached to the cross-shaft, so they push the sun gears round, which turns the driveshafts to drive the wheels, and the whole unit rotates as one. When the car turns a corner, the inner wheel will slow down, and cause the planet gears to turn on their own axis to speed up the outer wheel, but both wheels still receive the same amount of driving power.

When to change transmission oil

Manual transmissions

The oil change intervals are usually relatively infrequent (often around every 60,000 miles), and some transmissions are "sealed for life" and don't require any oil changes at all – you'll need to check your car manufacturer's service information, or check with an authorised dealer for details.

If your transmission has a level hole for checking the oil level (see "Fluids and filters"), you can get a rough idea of the oil's condition. Put on a pair of disposable gloves and dip your finger through the level hole into the oil. If you can't reach the oil, use a piece of bent wire instead. Pick up a few drops of oil, and drop them onto white paper.

Transmission oil is usually a clear, slightly yellowish colour, or sometimes clear reddish pink, depending on type. Unlike engine oil, transmission oil doesn't tend to blacken with age. If the oil is heavily discoloured, or if there are signs of metal particles in it, it should be changed.

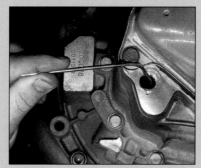

Automatic transmissions

If the fluid isn't changed at the recommended intervals it can cause serious and expensive problems. To get an idea of the condition of the fluid, pull out the fluid level dipstick, and drip a few drops of fluid onto white paper.

• Clear, pinkish red – fluids have different colours, but if it looks clean and has an obvious colour, it's probably OK.
• Dark, reddish brown – if the fluid looks and smells burnt, it needs changing.
• Milky white, pinkish – could be a leak in the fluid cooler allowing coolant to mix with the fluid. Have the problem checked as soon as possible.
• Metal particles – this could be serious. Some metal debris is normal after a high mileage, so have the fluid and filter changed, then re-check after a few thousand miles. If you can still see debris, take the car for a thorough check.

Running gear

The term "running gear" refers to the various components and systems which between them determine the car's ride, roadholding and stopping capability: tyres, wheels, brakes, steering and suspension. All these items interact with each other to some extent - even something as simple as fitting a different make of tyre can produce surprising differences in handling and noise.

Very early cars adopted the solid tyres, beam axles and cart springs used on the horse-drawn conveyances which they were about to supersede. Brakes, too, were primitive contraptions of limited capability. Rapid improvements followed, with a good deal of ingenuity being brought to bear the resolve the sometimes conflicting demands of good roadholding and comfort.

Nowadays we take for granted features such as power-assisted steering and reliable, effective brakes. Perhaps the most dramatic change in recent years has been the widespread adoption of anti-lock braking (ABS), made possible by the availability of cheap microprocessors. The same technology has also been used by some manufacturers to control smart suspension systems, and further developments will no doubt follow.

Steering

The steering's job is obvious, but steering systems have to be carefully designed to work in conjunction with the suspension. The steering system must allow the driver to keep the car pointing straight-ahead, even when hitting bumps at high speed, and the driver must be able to steer the car without too much effort.

When the steering wheel is turned, if the front wheels both turn through exactly the same angle, the tyres will tend to scrub and wear out very quickly. This is because for the car to turn in a circle, the wheel on the inside of the turn needs to turn through a larger angle than the wheel on the outside of the turn. The steering and front suspension are designed to allow this to happen.

Many cars are fitted with power steering, to reduce the effort required to turn the steering wheel.

Most power steering systems use hydraulic pressure to increase the effort applied by the driver. An engine-driven pump supplies the hydraulic pressure. The system has to be carefully designed so that the amount of assistance is proportional to the amount of effort applied by the driver, and the driver can still "feel" what's happening to the front wheels.

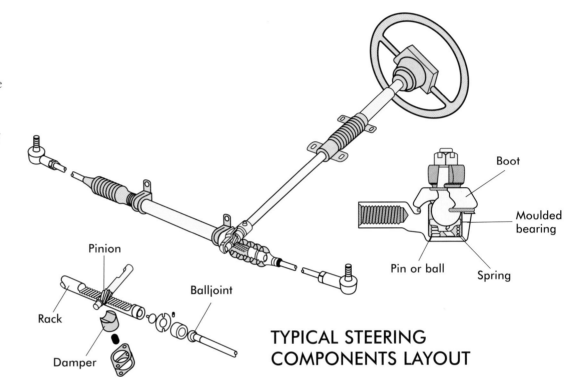

TYPICAL STEERING COMPONENTS LAYOUT

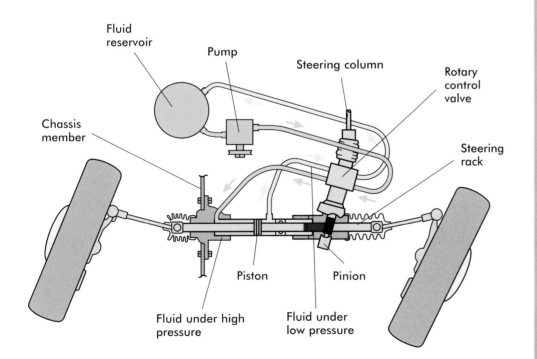

TYPICAL POWER STEERING SYSTEM LAYOUT

Steering problems

Basically, the same comments made under "Suspension problems" apply to the steering. The most common problem is poor front wheel alignment, which can cause tyre wear (see "Tyre wear").

Worn steering components can cause excessive free play at the steering wheel, and if you notice this problem, it should be dealt with as soon as possible.

Problems with power steering are usually due to leaks or air in the hydraulic system, or an incorrectly adjusted or broken pump drivebelt. If the power steering fails, the steering will still work, but the steering wheel will be harder to turn.

If you think there may be a problem with the steering, have it checked as soon as possible – never take any risks where the steering is concerned.

Suspension

The suspension serves two basic purposes; it keeps the tyres in contact with the road, enabling the driver to control the car, and it cushions the car's occupants from bumps and pot-holes in the road.

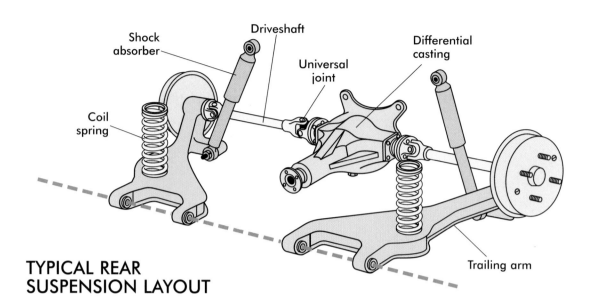

TYPICAL REAR SUSPENSION LAYOUT

The design of the suspension is always a compromise, because the characteristics needed to give a comfortable ride generally won't give good handling, and vice versa. For a comfortable ride, a reasonably soft suspension is needed to cushion the body from imperfections in the road surface. For good handling, a stiff suspension is needed to keep all four tyres in contact with the road, and to keep the body as still as possible.

Many older cars had independent front suspension, and a solid rear axle, whilst most modern cars have independent suspension all-round. On cars with a solid rear axle, when the rear wheel on one side of the car moves, it directly affects the other rear wheel.

The suspension on most conventional cars uses a combination of springs and shock absorbers to help absorb road shocks. An anti-roll bar may be used to resist the tendency of the body to "roll" when cornering. The suspension components are mounted on the body using rubbers to reduce the transmission of shocks, noise and vibration from the suspension to the body.

Suspension systems are very carefully and precisely designed, and the springs and shock absorbers are carefully chosen according to the weight and handling characteristics of the particular model of car.

Worn or damaged suspension components will affect the handling and braking of the car, and can be very dangerous.

Suspension problems

If the suspension components are worn or damaged, you'll probably notice that the handling and ride will suffer, and you may notice noises and rattles, especially when driving over bumps. Worn suspension components can also cause increased tyre wear, and poor braking.

The suspension components are very accurately aligned, and even a small tap to a wheel from "kerbing" can knock out the alignment and cause tyre wear. Many tyre specialists will be able to check the alignment for you.

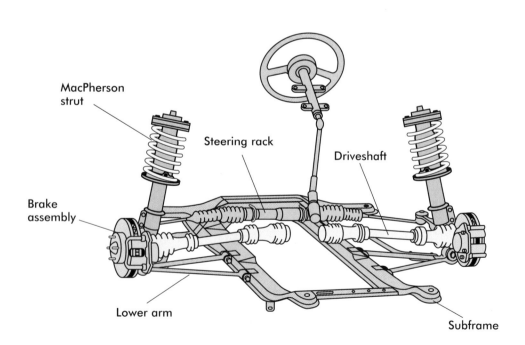

TYPICAL FRONT SUSPENSION LAYOUT

Shock absorbers

When one of the car's wheels hits a bump, the suspension spring is compressed, and when the bump has passed, the spring rebounds back past its rest position and starts to bounce around, or oscillate. This effect will make the car's occupants feel sea-sick, and will affect the handling. Shock absorbers are fitted to absorb the energy from the springs, which stops unwanted oscillations.

Most shock absorbers are designed to be "double-acting" which means that they resist movement to "bump" and "rebound". Shock absorbers are usually oil or gas-filled, and they consist of a piston, a cylinder and a reservoir. The end of the piston rod is usually connected to the body, and the lower end of the cylinder is usually connected to the suspension.

What happens when they wear out?

When shock absorbers wear, it will cause poor handling and braking because the body will move more than usual, and the wheels will tend to bounce when they hit bumps. Driving a car with worn shock absorbers can be very dangerous, and many tyre and exhaust specialists offer a shock absorber fitting service at very reasonable cost.

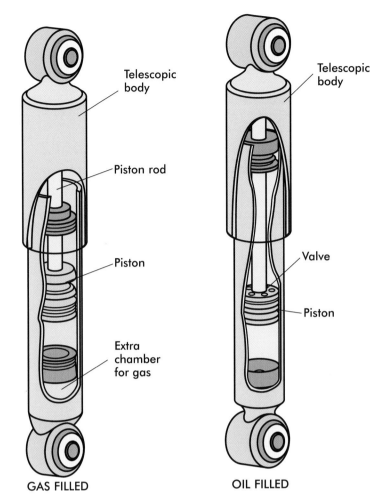

CUTAWAY VIEWS OF TYPICAL SHOCK ABSORBERS

How to check shock absorbers

Press down and then release each corner of the car in turn. The corner of the car should move back up to its original position, and then settle. If the suspension rises up and bounces when you let go, or if you hear a hissing or knocking sound as the suspension moves, the shock absorber is probably faulty.

Tyres

The importance of tyres is often overlooked, the only contact with the road is through the tyres. They must be free from damage, correctly inflated, and must have enough tread to give the necessary grip. Check the correct pressures with your car's handbook. Note that pressures should be checked when the tyres are cold (not driven for at least 30 minutes), and that the pressures may be different for front and rear tyres, and also for fully loaded conditions. The pressure marked on the side of the tyre is the maximum, not the running pressure.

Checking tyres

Taking each wheel in turn, unscrew the valve dust cap and put it somewhere safe.

Check the tyre pressure by pushing the nozzle of the gauge firmly on to the valve so that no air can be heard escaping. Remove the gauge from the valve and check the reading.

If the pressure needs increasing slightly, you can drive to the nearest garage, or use your pump according to the instructions.

Check the pressure again. If it's now too high, gently press the pin in the centre of the tyre valve to release a small quantity of air at a time. Re-check the pressure with the gauge. Refit the dust cap when you've finished.

Don't forget the spare tyre just because it's out of sight. Inflate this to the highest of the pressures quoted for your car.

All tyres must have at least the minimum legal amount of tread - that's 1.6 mm in the UK, although in practice it's better to change tyres well before they become this worn. Use a tread depth gauge according to the instructions to check the tread remaining.

Ideally you should also check the general condition of each tyre. You'll need to jack up each wheel in turn and rotate it. Look for any damage, bulges, or foreign bodies in treads or sidewalls, and for uneven tread wear, indicating possible wheel misalignment. If you find any of these, drive carefully to the tyre specialist for further advice.

Tyre wear

No matter how well you look after your tyres, they'll wear out eventually. It's difficult to say what constitutes a normal life expectancy, because individual conditions vary so much. What is certain is that neglecting or abusing tyres will definitely shorten their life. The way in which tyres wear can provide clues to possible problems.

Shoulder wear

Under-inflation (wear on both sides)	Under-inflation will cause overheating of the tyre, because the tyre will flex too much, and the tread will not sit correctly on the road surface. This will cause a loss of grip and excessive wear, not to mention the danger of sudden tyre failure due to heat build-up. Check and adjust pressures.
Incorrect wheel camber (wear on one side)	Repair or renew suspension parts.
Hard cornering	Reduce speed!

Centre wear

Over-inflation	Over-inflation will cause rapid wear of the centre part of the tyre tread, along with reduced grip, harsher ride, and the danger of shock damage occurring in the tyre casing. Check and adjust pressures.

Uneven wear

Front tyres may wear unevenly as a result of wheel misalignment. Most tyre dealers and garages can check and adjust the wheel alignment (or "tracking") for a modest charge.

Incorrect camber or castor	Repair or renew suspension parts.
Incorrect toe-setting	Adjust front wheel alignment.

Note: The feathered edge of the tread which typifies toe wear is best checked by feel – run your fingers across the tyre tread.

Unbalanced wheel	Balance wheels.
Malfunctioning suspension	Repair or renew suspension parts.

Tyre size markings

All tyres carry standard tyre size markings on their sidewalls, such as **"185/70 R 13 87T"**.

185 indicates the width of the tyre in mm.

70 indicates the ratio of the tyre section height to width, expressed as a percentage. If no number is present at this point, the ratio is considered to be 82%.

R indicates the tyre is of radial ply construction.

13 indicates the wheel diameter for the tyre is 13 inches.

87 is an index number which indicates the maximum load that the tyre can carry at maximum speed.

T represents the maximum speed for the tyre which should be equal to or greater than the car's maximum speed.

Note that some tyres have the speed rating symbol located between the tyre width and the wheel diameter, attached to the "R" radial tyre reference, for example, "185/70 HR 13".

Speed rating symbols for radial tyres

Symbol	km/h	mph
P	150	93
Q	160	99
R	170	106
S	180	112
T	190	118
U	200	124
V (after size markings)	Up to 240	Up to 150
H (within size markings)	Up to 210	Up to 130
V (within size markings)	Over 210	Over 130
Z (within size markings)	Over 240	Over 150

How to choose a new tyre

Buying the cheapest tyres can be a false economy. Some budget tyres are just as capable as branded tyres, but beware of very cheap imports and re-manufactured tyres.

Don't buy second-hand (so-called "part worn") tyres. They may have suffered accident or other damage which will not necessarily be visible externally.

Make sure you buy the correct size and speed rating of tyre (see "Tyre size markings").

The tyre tread pattern can affect the way the car handles, so if possible always match the tread patterns, ie, if you're having a new front left-hand tyre fitted, try to make sure that it's of the same type and tread pattern as the front right-hand tyre. (This is a legal requirement in many countries.) Tyres with different tread patterns may cause the car to pull to one side when braking, or one side may have less grip on a slippery surface.

The tyres on the driven wheels usually wear more quickly than those on the undriven wheels (especially on front-wheel-drive cars). You can even out the wear by "rotating" the tyres every few thousand miles, which means swapping the front tyres with the rear, and vice versa.

If you do a lot of driving in slippery conditions, it may be worth buying a separate set of wheels, and having M+S (Mud and Snow) tyres fitted.

Forever pumping up a tyre?

Check that the valve dust cap isn't missing, and if it is buy a new one and fit it as soon as possible.

If the valve cap is in place and the tyre's losing air, it could be due to a leaky valve. If the valve's leaking badly, you'll be able to hear a hissing sound. If you can't hear any sound, put a little soapy water around the edge of the valve – a leak will tend to produce air bubbles. Even if none of these checks shows up a problem with the valve, it could still be faulty, but the leak may be so slow that you can't detect it.

Another possible cause of trouble is a slow puncture. This could be due to poor sealing between the tyre and the wheel, or a foreign object may be stuck in the tyre.

There's a nail in my tyre!

If you find a nail, or any similar foreign body, in your tyre, don't pull it out as it marks the puncture location. Fit the spare wheel straight away (see "In an emergency"), then take the damaged tyre to a tyre specialist.

If the tyre's not too worn, it will be worth having it repaired; otherwise, you'll have to buy a new tyre. The tyre specialist will advise you.

Buying a tyre pump

There are two basic types of pump: foot pumps and electric pumps. The easiest type of pump to use is an electric one, with a built-in gauge, that plugs into the car's cigarette lighter.

Foot pumps come in various shapes and sizes, and basically you get what you pay for. If you can afford it, it's best to buy a pump with a metal barrel because it will be more robust. Bear in mind that the bigger the pump, the easier it will be to blow up a tyre!

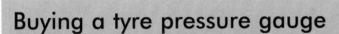

Buying a tyre pressure gauge

Pressure gauges come in various patterns: plunger-types, dial gauges, and electronic (digital) gauges. Which one you choose is really down to personal preference, but the easiest type of gauge to use is a dial-type.

High quality, high accuracy gauges can be expensive, but you don't need to spend a fortune. As long as your gauge is reasonably accurate and robust, it should serve you well.

Note that even if the pump you're using has a built-in pressure gauge, it's always best to check the pressure with a separate gauge. The gauges built into pumps can be inaccurate, and are easily damaged when using the pump. Likewise, the gauges attached to garage air lines are notoriously inaccurate. By all means use the air line to inflate your tyres, but use your own gauge to check the pressure afterwards.

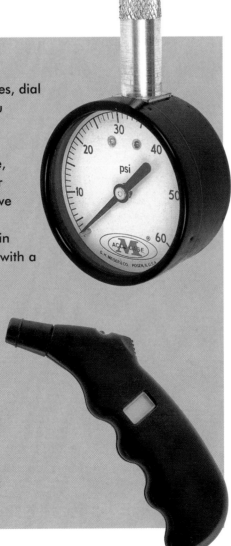

Wheels

Spoked wheels aren't seen very much these days, which is just as well - they looked pretty, but they were expensive to produce and difficult to maintain, as anyone who has tried to true-up a bicycle wheel will testify.

The wheels on modern cars are made of pressed steel or aluminium; they are strong, light and sometimes decorative, but they still need a certain amount of looking after, mostly for cosmetic reasons.

Cleaning steel wheels and covers

Cleaning with car shampoo and a sponge should give acceptable results. Any stubborn dirt can be removed using a brush, and if necessary a wheel cleaner spray (check that it's suitable for use on plastic components, if applicable – most alloy wheel cleaners aren't).

Cleaning alloy wheels

Using an alloy wheel cleaner solution and a soft-bristled brush should get rid of most of the dirt. Always follow the instructions on the packaging when using wheel cleaner – some cleaners are caustic, in which case wear gloves, and don't get the cleaner on the car's paintwork.

Once you've got alloy wheels clean, polishing them will make dirt easier to remove in the future. You can use a special alloy wheel polish, or if your wheels have a clear-coat finish applied over the metal, ordinary wax car polish will give good results.

WARNING

When you're cleaning wheels, take care not to breathe in brake dust, as it can be dangerous to health.

Touching-up alloy wheels

Most alloy wheels have a clear-coat finish applied to the metal. If the clear-coat finish gets chipped, it's a good idea to repair the chipped area before the exposed alloy becomes stained or oxidised.

1 Clean the wheel using alloy wheel cleaner, then rinse the wheel and thoroughly dry it.

2 Clean and polish the exposed alloy using fine (400-grade) emery paper, or a fine scouring pad. Carefully feather the edges of the clear-coat surrounding the affected area, then wipe clean with a dry cloth.

3 Use a fine artist's brush to apply the clear-coat (follow the preparation instructions on the packaging). Apply several thin coats to blend in with the surrounding area.

Removing a wheel?

Although it's important for safety to make sure that the wheel bolts or nuts are tight, you need to be able to unscrew them so that you can change the wheel if you have a puncture (see "How to change a wheel").

1 If your car has locking wheel bolts or nuts, always make sure that you carry the adapter in the car in case you have to change a wheel.

2 Carry a wheel brace with an extending handle to make it easier to unscrew the wheel bolts/nuts.

• If you've had a new tyre fitted, check that you can still unscrew the wheel bolts or nuts. Slacken them, then retighten them to make sure.

• Ideally, the wheel bolts or nuts should be tightened to the manufacturer's specified torque. If you don't have a torque wrench, you could ask your local garage to tighten the bolts or nuts for you.

3 Before refitting a wheel, clean the wheel bolt or nut threads with a wire brush. Smear the threads with anti-seize compound (available from a motor factor or car accessory shop), or a little general-purpose grease.

How to avoid losing wheel covers

Unclip the wheel cover, and check for any broken clips. If a clip is badly broken, or if several clips are broken, you may have no option but to renew the cover.

Buy a few long cable-ties, of a colour suitable for your wheel covers. If the wheel covers have holes in them, feed a cable-tie through one of the holes in the cover. Loop the cable-tie round behind the wheel, and push it back out through another suitable hole in the wheel cover.

Fasten the ends of the cable-tie together, then pull tight, and cut off the excess.

You can hide the joined ends of the cable-tie by sliding the cable-tie round so that the ends are behind the wheel cover.

If your wheel trims don't have any holes, you can still secure them using cable-ties, but secure the cable-ties to the clips on the back of the wheel covers.

Remember that the wheel cover will have to be removed to change the wheel, so carry a suitable tool to cut the cable tie.

Brakes

Early cars had mechanical (cable- or rod-operated) brakes. As braking technology improved, hydraulic braking systems were introduced. All modern cars have hydraulic brakes.

The hydraulic system multiplies the pressure applied to the brake pedal, to give a much higher pressure at each brake. Hydraulic fluid can't be compressed. So, if the brake pedal operates a piston inside a master cylinder full of fluid connected to one end of a pipe (also full of fluid), this will move a second piston at the other end of the pipe, which can apply the brake. When a car is braking, about two-thirds of its weight acts on the front wheels, so the front brakes normally have bigger pistons than the rear ones.

If there's a leak in the hydraulic system, the fluid can escape when the pedal is pushed, so the brakes won't work properly. As a safety measure the hydraulic system is split into two separate circuits, with two pedal-operated pistons in a common master cylinder. Usually, each circuit operates one front brake and the diagonally-opposite rear brake, so that if one of the circuits develops a leak, the car will still stop in a straight line. Some systems are split front and rear, one circuit operating both front brakes, the other operating both rear brakes.

50kg force in master cylinder

75kg force in rear slave cylinder

HYDRAULIC CYLINDER OPERATION

150kg force in front slave cylinder

Foot applies force of 12kg

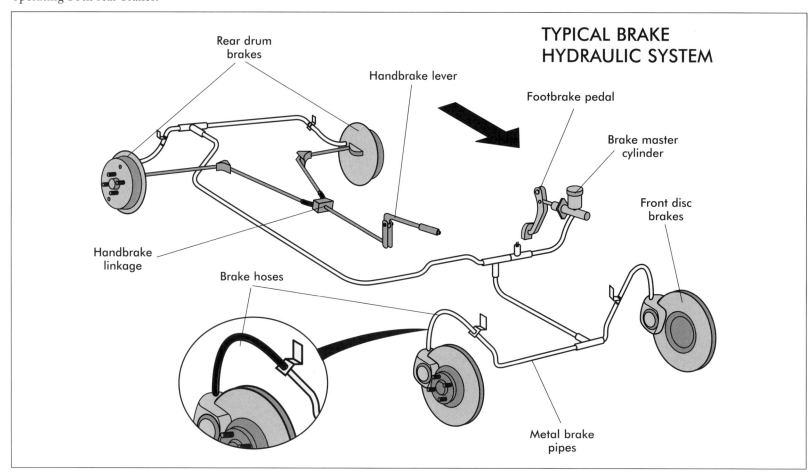

Rear drum brakes

Handbrake lever

TYPICAL BRAKE HYDRAULIC SYSTEM

Footbrake pedal

Brake master cylinder

Front disc brakes

Handbrake linkage

Brake hoses

Metal brake pipes

Disc brakes

Front disc brakes are used on all modern cars, and disc brakes are also often used at the rear.

A disc brake assembly consists of a caliper and a disc. The caliper incorporates one or two hydraulic cylinders and pistons and carries two brake pads. The caliper straddles the disc, and is mounted on a fixed part of the front suspension. The disc is fixed to the rotating hub which turns with the wheel.

Two basic types of caliper are used:

• **A fixed caliper** usually has two pistons, one located on each side of the disc. The caliper can't move, and the brake pedal pressure operates both pistons simultaneously.

• **A sliding caliper** usually has one piston, normally located on the inboard side of the brake disc. The caliper is free to slide, and when the caliper piston is operated, it pushes the inner brake pad against the disc. Once the pad touches the disc, the caliper piston can't move any further, so it pushes the cylinder away from the piston, which moves the caliper inwards, and pulls the outer brake pad against the disc. Now both pads are clamped against the disc.

Each brake pad consists of a metal backing plate, with friction material bonded to it. Eventually the friction material will wear away, and the pads will have to be replaced.

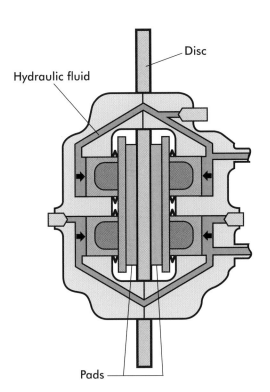

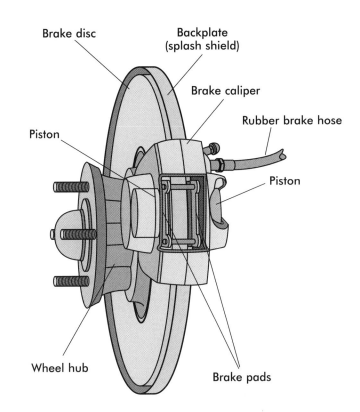

TYPICAL DISC BRAKE COMPONENTS

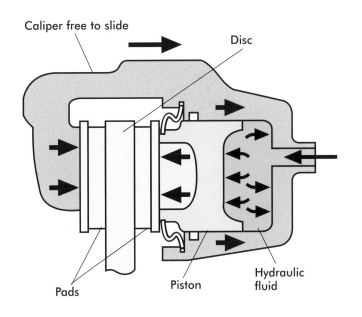

FIXED CALIPER OPERATION

SLIDING CALIPER OPERATION

Drum brakes

Rear drum brakes are used on many modern cars, and on older cars they were used at the front as well.

A drum brake assembly consists of a wheel cylinder, two brake shoes, a backplate and a drum. The drum is fixed to the rotating hub which turns with the wheel. The brake shoes fit inside the drum, and are curved, with friction material on their outer faces. The shoes are mounted on the backplate, which is itself mounted on a fixed part of the rear suspension. One end of each shoe rests against an anchor point, which acts as a pivot. The other end is pushed outwards by the piston in the wheel cylinder when the brake pedal is pressed, and contacts the inner surface of the drum, braking the drum and wheel. When the brakes are released, return springs stretched between the two shoes pull them away from the drum, which allows the drum and the wheel to turn freely.

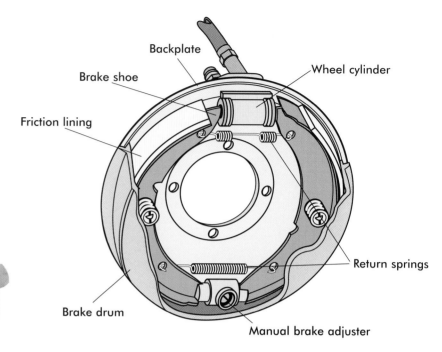

Backplate
Brake shoe
Wheel cylinder
Friction lining
Return springs
Brake drum
Manual brake adjuster

DRUM BRAKE OPERATION

Servo-assisted brakes

A heavy car needs a high pedal pressure to give maximum braking power. Using a vacuum-operated servo reduces the pedal pressure exerted by the driver. The servo has a vacuum chamber connected to a vacuum source. A diaphragm in the servo chamber is connected to a pushrod, which operates the master cylinder pistons. When the brake pedal is pressed, air flows into the chamber behind the diaphragm, and because there's a vacuum on the other side, the air pushes the diaphragm forwards, operating the brakes. The amount of assistance is proportional to the pressure applied to the brake pedal.

If the servo develops a fault, the brakes will still work, but the driver will have to press the pedal much harder to achieve the same result.

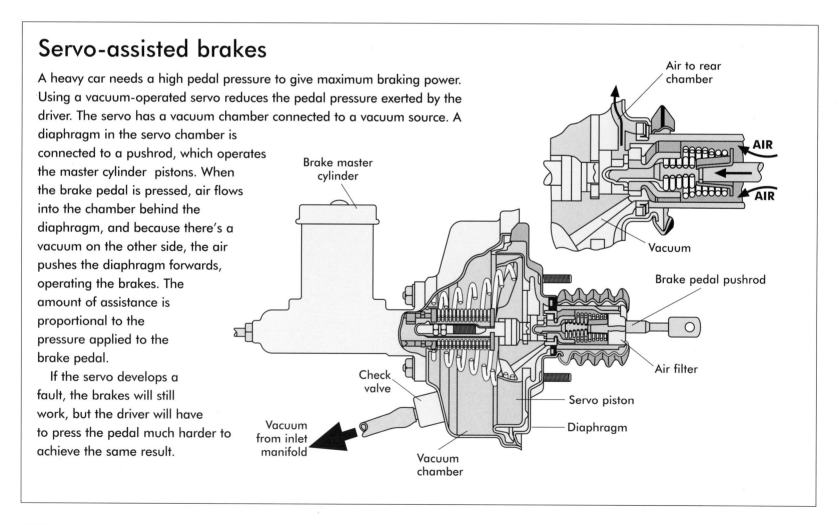

Air to rear chamber
AIR
AIR
Vacuum
Brake master cylinder
Brake pedal pushrod
Air filter
Check valve
Servo piston
Diaphragm
Vacuum from inlet manifold
Vacuum chamber

Anti-lock Braking Systems (ABS)

Anti-lock Braking Systems (ABS) are designed to stop wheels from locking under heavy braking. Some systems, mainly the early types, work only on the front wheels, but most systems work on all four wheels.

ABS works by detecting when a particular wheel is about to lock. It then reduces the hydraulic pressure applied to that wheel's brake, releasing it just before the wheel locks, and then re-applies it.

The system consists of a hydraulic unit, which contains various solenoid valves and an electric fluid return pump, four roadwheel sensors, and an electronic control unit (ECU). The solenoids in the hydraulic unit are controlled by the ECU, which receives signals from the four wheel sensors.

If the ECU senses that a wheel is about to lock, it operates the relevant solenoid valve in the hydraulic unit, which isolates that brake from the master cylinder. If the wheel sensor detects that the wheel is still about to lock, the ECU switches on the fluid return pump in the hydraulic unit and pumps the fluid back from the brake to the master cylinder, releasing the brake. Once the speed of the wheel returns to normal, the return pump stops and the solenoid valve opens, allowing fluid pressure back to the brake, and so the brake is re-applied. This whole cycle can be repeated many times a second. The rapid variations in fluid pressure cause pulses in the hydraulic circuit, and these can be felt through the brake pedal.

The wheel sensors are usually mounted on a fixed part of the

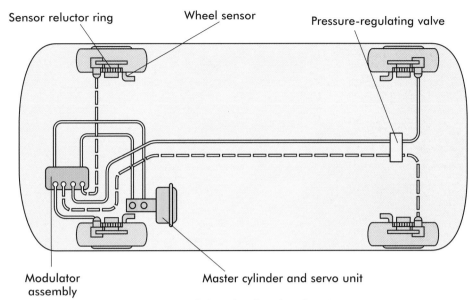

Sensor reluctor ring   Wheel sensor   Pressure-regulating valve

Modulator assembly   Master cylinder and servo unit

TYPICAL ABS LAYOUT

suspension, and use a toothed rotor fixed to the wheel hub to monitor the speed of the wheel.

The system relies totally on electrical signals. If an inaccurate signal or a battery problem is detected, the ABS is automatically shut down, and a warning light on the instrument panel will come on. Normal braking will always be available whether or not the ABS is working.

ABS cannot work miracles, and the basic laws of physics will still apply: stopping distances will always be greater on slippery surfaces. The greatest benefit of ABS is being able to brake hard in an emergency without having to worry about correcting a skid.

If you have any problems with an ABS, always consult an authorised dealer.

Brake fluid

Brake fluid deteriorates with age because it absorbs moisture from the atmosphere. If the system has even a small amount of moisture in it, the brakes won't work as well as they could, and you might notice that the brake pedal has a "spongy" feel (this could also be due to air in the system).

Moisture can also attack the rubber seals in the system. To prevent these problems, it's important to have the brake fluid renewed at the recommended intervals (see "Fluids and filters").

Note that certain Citroen cars use a special hydraulic fluid (LHM). LHM has many advantages over conventional brake fluid, but it still needs renewing at regular intervals.

Handbrake

The handbrake (parking brake) is usually operated by pulling a lever. The handbrake usually works on the rear wheels, although a few cars have a front wheel handbrake.

If rear drum brakes are fitted, the handbrake operates the same shoes as the footbrake, using cables and levers to push the shoes against the drum.

Several different handbrake systems are used on cars with disc brakes. Some systems use small additional drum brakes, some use two additional pads, and others use a mechanical linkage to operate the main caliper pistons.

Almost all types of handbrake have adjustment to allow for friction material wear and handbrake cable stretch.

Windows, wipers and mirrors

The first motorists had no problems with keeping their car windows clear, for the simple reason that there were no windows. (In the absence of safety glass that was probably no bad thing.) Today's drivers don't have to cope with their goggles steaming up, but an occasional window-cleaning session is recommended. If you haven't cleaned your car's windows for some time, you may be surprised at the difference.

Windscreen wiper blades tend to be neglected until they are literally falling to pieces, and exterior mirrors are all too easily damaged. These problems are easy to fix, as the following pages show.

Wipers

It's a good idea to check the wiper blades regularly for damage and wear. Correctly working windscreen wipers are an important safety item as well as a legal requirement. If they tend to smear, or fail to clear water from the screen, the wiper blades probably need to be renewed.

If you're on a tight budget, it's possible to buy replacement rubbers only, but to fit these, you need to dismantle the blade, and this can be very fiddly. It's advisable to renew the whole blade because the springs and hinges weaken with age.

You can buy new wiper blades from an authorised dealer for your car, or from most motor factors and car accessory shops. When you go to buy new blades, you'll need to know the make, model, and the year of manufacture of your car.

As you remove the old wiper blade, note carefully how it's fitted, to help when fitting the new blade.

Fitting a new wiper blade

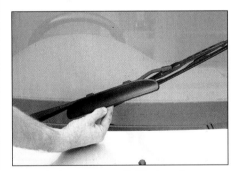

1 With the ignition off, lift the wiper arm until it locks in the upright position. If the arm won't lock in position, hold it until you can remove the blade; take care not to allow the arm to spring back.

2 To remove the blade, first turn it at right-angles to the arm. Press the securing tab(s), where fitted, then slide the blade out of the hooked end of the arm.

3 Fit the adapter to the new blade (look on the packet for details).

4 Fit the blade to the arm, making sure that it's fully home. Lower the arm gently onto the screen. Check that the wipers work before driving the car.

Looking after your wiper blades

◆ Carefully lift the wiper arm from the windscreen (take care not to allow it to spring back against the glass), then wipe the cleaning edge of the blade with a clean cloth dipped in screenwash concentrate. Check the blade rubber carefully for damage. If you find cracks or tears, renew the blade.

◆ When laying the blade back in position on the glass, make sure that it's pushing on the glass correctly. If the blade pushes on the glass too hard, it will squeak and may cause smearing, and if the blade doesn't push hard enough, it won't clear the glass effectively. This sort of problem is normally cured by fitting new wiper arms.

◆ If the blades don't wipe the screen properly, renew them, even if they look OK. It's a good idea to renew the wiper blades once a year in any case, preferably before the start of winter.

◆ When using the wipers to clear the screen, always make sure that the screen is wet. Don't use a higher wiper speed than you need when it's raining, and if your car has separate switches for the washers and wipers, always make sure that you operate the washers to wet the screen before switching on the wipers.

◆ In winter, if you switch on the wipers with the blades frozen in place, you can quickly burn out the wiper motor, which could be an expensive mistake. Frozen wiper blades can usually be freed using de-icer – if you pull the blades from a frozen screen take care not to tear the rubbers.

Windscreen and windows

It's essential for safety that the driver can see clearly through all the car's windows. If the glass is clean, you'll be able to see better, and it won't fog up as quickly. Always make sure that the washer fluid reservoir is full, that the windscreen wipers work, and that the wiper blades are clean.

Dazzle and reflections

You may find that your windscreen looks perfectly clean during the day, but at night you get distracting reflections and dazzle from car headlights. This is often due to a greasy film on the inside of the glass, or smears where the glass has been wiped. The demister may not have much effect on this greasy film, and it's a good idea to keep a sponge pad or a small chamois leather in the car to wipe the inside of the glass.

The plastic trim inside cars gives off vapours, and they often leave a greasy film on the inside of the glass. If you or your passengers smoke, this can also cause a deposit to form on the glass. Here are a couple of tips to help relieve the problem.

● Wash the inside of the windows with an ammonia-based glass cleaner. Screenwash additive often contains ammonia (check on the bottle), so try wiping the glass with a concentrated screenwash solution.

● Clean the plastic trim with a detergent solution (a few drops of washing-up liquid in a bowl of water). Use this sparingly - you don't want to splash water into any electrical components.

● Rinse off the plastic trim with a cloth dipped in plain water, then dry the surfaces with clean cloths. Leave the car windows open until the trim has dried thoroughly.

Smeary windscreen?

If your windscreen smears, the first thing to check is the wiper blades (see "Wipers"). Smearing is quite common if the blades are old, or in cold weather when the rubber will tend to harden. You might also find that the blades will smear if they are pressing too hard on the glass.

Smearing is also a common problem when driving on motorways due to the build-up of diesel particles and general traffic grime. Always make sure you keep the washer fluid reservoir topped up, and always use a screenwash additive.

What should I use to clean the glass?

You can use household glass cleaners on car windows, but check that they won't damage the plastic trim or paint. Some household cleaners are very watery, and will run off the glass before you get a chance to use your cloth!

To wipe the glass, a soft lint-free cloth will usually do a better job than a paper towel. Keep a small sponge or a chamois leather in the car to wipe away condensation and smears.

Driving in damp or wintry weather

If your car windows are misted up or iced over, never be tempted to drive off peering through a small hole. Start the engine, switch on the demister and heated rear window and wait for the windows to clear, or wipe or scrape the windows clean before you start your journey. Remember, it's not just the windscreen that needs to be clear, you need to be able to see through all the windows.

You also need to be able to see clearly in all the mirrors. If your car has heated mirrors, switch them on; if not, scrape off ice or wipe off condensation before you drive off.

If the outside of your windscreen is dirty, the headlights are probably dirty too. Unless your car has a headlight washer system, check the lights, and clean them if necessary, at least once a week or before a long journey. In really foul conditions you may need to clean the headlights every time you stop.

Leaky windscreen

If the windscreen leaks, it's not only annoying, it can also ruin carpets and trim, and it can lead to electrical trouble if water seeps down into the wiring behind the dashboard.

On some cars, the windscreen may be fixed in place using a rubber seal, but on most modern cars the windscreen is bonded directly to the body using a special adhesive, with no seal.

If your windscreen has a rubber seal, check that the rubber isn't damaged or perished – if it is, you'll need to have the rubber renewed (a windscreen specialist will be able to do this for you), which should cure the leak.

If the rubber seal seems to be in good condition, or if you've got a bonded windscreen, you should be able to cure the leak using a clear silicone sealant (available from motor factors and car accessory shops). Carefully clean around the leaky area. If a rubber seal is fitted, carefully prise up both edges of the seal, and work sealant in under the rubber – if the sealant spout is small enough, push it under the rubber and slide it along the glass whilst squeezing the sealant into place. If your car has a bonded windscreen, carefully apply a small bead of sealant under the edges of the windscreen trim and/or to the joint between the windscreen and the body. You can remove any excess when it's dried, using a sharp knife.

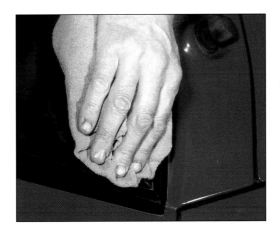

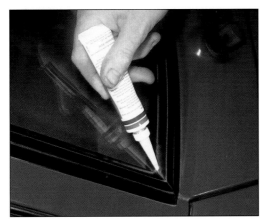

My heated rear window doesn't work

If your car's heated rear window doesn't work at all, check the security of the electrical connectors on each side of the window. If they're OK, check the fuse (refer to your car's handbook to find out where it is) and renew it if necessary. If the fuse blows again, or if it wasn't blown in the first place, you'll have to ask a garage or a car electrical specialist to investigate the problem.

Sometimes one or more of the individual heating wires may not be working. This is caused by small breaks in the wires - they are quite fragile and are easily damaged by over-enthusiastic cleaning or by having luggage rubbing against them. You can buy special conductive paint to repair these breaks. Use the paint as directed by the manufacturer.

Cracks and scratches

Cracks and scratches in the windscreen can be a distraction and a worry, but if the damage isn't too deep, there may be a way of getting rid of it without the need for a new windscreen.

You might be able to polish out light scratches with glass polish, toothpaste or jewellers' polishing compound. Try putting a little on a clean cloth, and rub it repeatedly over the damaged area, then wash off the residue.

If you haven't had any success polishing out the damage, it's worth asking a windscreen repair specialist to take a look. A skilled specialist may be able to polish out the scratch using an industrial polish, or special tools.

Stone chips and small cracks can also often be repaired by windscreen repair specialists.

If a crack or stone chip cannot be repaired, provided that the damage is not directly in the driver's line of vision, it may not be necessary to have a new windscreen fitted straight away. Don't leave large cracks or chips too long without having them repaired, it may only take a large bump in the road or a stone hitting the windscreen to turn a crack or chip into a much bigger problem!

If you are unfortunate enough to break a windscreen, refer to "In an emergency" for advice.

Fitting a new door mirror glass

If just the mirror glass itself is broken, you can probably find a suitable self-adhesive replacement from a motor factor or car accessory shop. If you can't find a suitable replacement glass, you should be able to buy one from an authorised dealer for your particular car, but you may have to ask for advice on how to fit the new glass. Most glasses clip into place, but there are several different types of clip, and the new glass is easily broken if you use the wrong fitting method!

If the mirror housing is damaged, or if the mirror glass is heated, you'll need to buy the appropriate replacement parts from an authorised dealer, and you may have to have the new parts fitted professionally.

1 If the original mirror glass is cracked, but otherwise intact, carefully clean the glass to remove all traces of dirt and grease (take care not to cut yourself on sharp edges).

2 If the original mirror glass is broken, and pieces of glass are missing, carefully prise out and remove the remaining glass, and clean off any old adhesive.

3 Follow the instructions supplied with the new mirror glass. You may just need to peel a backing sheet from the rear of the new glass and press the glass into position, or the new glass may be supplied with double-sided self-adhesive pads. In either case, make sure that the glass is correctly aligned before pressing it firmly into position.

4 Don't forget to clean your finger marks off the new mirror glass!

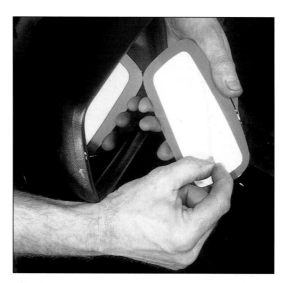

Adjusting the washer spray

Before assuming that the washer needs to be adjusted, check that the nozzle isn't partially blocked. A partial blockage can cause the spray to be deflected.

Most nozzles have a small ball jet, and these can be adjusted by poking a stout pin into the end of the nozzle, and using the pin to lever the nozzle round. Take care not to break the pin off in the nozzle.

To adjust some types of nozzle, you'll have to bend the nozzle itself using a pair of pliers, whilst other types of nozzle, such as those attached to the wiper blades, are not adjustable.

Normally, when the car's parked, you need to aim the jets slightly high, because the airflow when the car's moving will tend to deflect the spray down.

Re-attaching an interior mirror

If your interior rear view mirror falls off, it's not only annoying, it's dangerous, and it's illegal to drive with no mirror. You will need masking tape, glass cleaner, a clean cloth, a double-sided mirror fixing pad (available from car accessory shops).

1 Mark the location of the mirror on the outside of the windscreen using masking tape, then thoroughly clean the inside of the glass to remove all traces of old adhesive and dirt. Allow the glass to dry.

2 Similarly, remove all traces of old adhesive and dirt from the mirror mounting bracket.

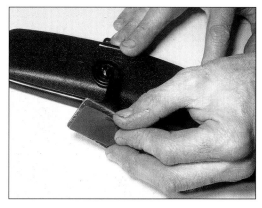

3 Although some mirrors may be glued directly to the glass, it's easier to use a double-sided pad when carrying out a repair. Peel off the backing sheet from one side of the new mirror fixing pad, then push the pad firmly into position on the mirror mounting bracket.

4 Make sure that the windscreen is dry (try not to breathe on the glass, which may cause misting), then peel the remaining backing sheet from the adhesive pad, and align the mounting bracket with the masking tape on the windscreen. Push the assembly firmly into position, and keep the pressure on for a few seconds. Don't try to move the assembly once you've pushed it into position.

5 If the mirror is separate from the mounting bracket, you can now slide the mirror into position on the bracket.

Blocked washer jet?

You can clear a blocked washer jet by poking the nozzle gently with a pin. Take care not to break the pin off in the nozzle.

Sometimes the washer jets can get blocked by contamination in the washer fluid. Residue can build up inside the washer fluid reservoir over a period of time, so it's worth cleaning out the reservoir once a year. If the reservoir is easily accessible, you can remove it and wash it out, otherwise you can flush it out using a hosepipe. It's a good idea to use a washer fluid additive, and in winter it's essential, otherwise the washers will freeze.

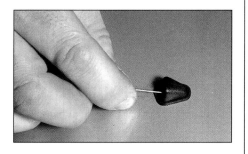

Electrical things

Electricity is a mystery to many people, perhaps because it cannot be seen. It may help to think of the battery as being like a water tank and the electricity as the "water" which flows down the wires in the same way as water flows down pipes - but, unlike water, electricity can flow uphill as easily as down.

Modern cars rely on their electrical systems not just for ignition, lighting and signalling, but also for controlling systems such as fuel injection and ABS. There's also the radio, the heated rear window, the heater blower, the central locking... in fact there are probably more fuses in your car's fusebox than there are in your house. This chapter takes the mystery out of some common electrical problems and gives you hints on some common operations like bulb and fuse renewal.

The electrical system

The electrical system on all modern cars consists of a 12-volt battery, an alternator, a starter motor, and various electrical accessories, components and wiring. Modern systems are all "negative earth" – this means that the battery negative lead is connected directly to the car's body, which cuts down on the wiring needed, and simplifies the layout of the electrical system.

The battery supplies electricity to operate the car's electrical systems when the engine isn't running, and when the electrical load exceeds the output from the alternator. It also has to provide electricity to operate the starter motor.

Once the engine is running, the alternator supplies the electricity to operate the various electrical systems (engine management system, lights, instruments, etc), and keeps the battery fully charged. The alternator is driven by a belt from the engine crankshaft pulley. The output from the alternator is carefully controlled so that it remains within certain limits whatever the speed of the engine.

On most starter motors, when the ignition key is turned to the start position, a solenoid moves the starter pinion into engagement with the engine's flywheel ring gear before the starter motor is energised. The motor is then energised to spin the flywheel until the engine starts. Once the engine has started, a one-way clutch prevents the motor being driven by the engine, until the pinion disengages from the flywheel.

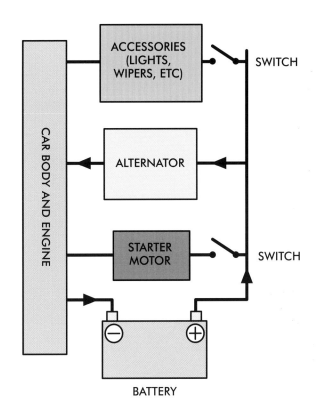

CAR ELECTRICAL SYSTEM

Precautions

It's necessary to take extra care when working on the electrical system to avoid damage to the components, and to avoid the risk of personal injury.

◆ Always remove rings, watches, etc before working on the electrical system. Even with the battery disconnected, you could get a nasty shock or burn if some component's live terminals are earthed through a metal object.

◆ Do not reverse the battery connections. Some components could be irreparably damaged.

◆ Never disconnect the battery terminals, the alternator, any electrical wiring or any test equipment when the engine is running.

◆ Don't allow the engine to turn the alternator when the alternator isn't connected.

◆ Always make sure that the battery negative lead is disconnected when working on the electrical system.

◆ The radio/cassette unit fitted as standard equipment may have a built-in security code to deter thieves. If the power source to the unit is cut, the anti-theft system will activate. Even if the power source is immediately reconnected, the radio/cassette unit won't work until the correct security code has been entered. So, if you don't know the correct security code for the radio/cassette unit don't disconnect the battery or remove the radio/cassette unit from the car.

Batteries

Always check your battery before the start of winter. During winter the battery is under extra strain when it has to start the car on cold, damp mornings. You're also likely to be using more electrical equipment in winter – heater, heated rear window, wipers, lights, etc.

How to check a battery

Make sure that the battery tray is in good condition, and that the securing clamp is tight. Corrosion can be removed with a solution of water and baking soda. Rinse with water. Any metal damaged by corrosion should be covered with a zinc-based primer, then painted.

1 Check the outside of the battery for damage. Check the tightness of the cable clamps to ensure good connections. You shouldn't be able to move them. Also check each cable for cracks and fraying.

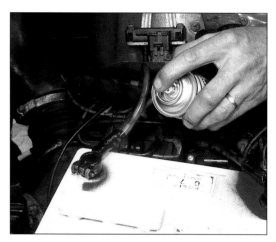

2 If the cable clamps are corroded (white fluffy deposits), disconnect the cables, clean them with a wire brush, then refit them. You can keep corrosion on the terminals to a minimum by applying petroleum jelly, or terminal protector, after reconnecting them.

Is the battery flat?

If the lights have been left on, you may find that there isn't enough power to turn the starter motor. You may even find that the warning lights don't come on when you turn the key.

The first sign of a failing battery is a sluggish starter motor. Turn on the headlights, and then operate the starter. If the headlights dim, or go out, it's probably a battery problem; it's worth getting the system checked by an auto-electrician.

If you have a test meter, you can test the battery output, but this will only be accurate if the battery has not been used for 6 hours. Connect the meter across the terminals (connecting the red lead to the positive terminal). If the battery is in good condition, the reading should be above 12.5 volts. If the reading is 12.2 to 12.4 volts, the battery is partially discharged, and if the reading is less than 12.2 volts, the battery is flat.

1. Call for assistance. If you're a member of one of the motoring breakdown organisations, they may even come to your house – check your membership documents for details.

2. Use jump leads to start the car – see "How to use jump leads".

3. Charge the battery – see "How to use a battery charger". You won't be able to start the car until the battery is charged, so if you want to use it straight away, you'll need to use one of the previous methods, then charge the battery later. If you drive the car a reasonable distance (say 20 miles or more), the alternator will charge the battery for you; fewer miles will mean the same starting problems next time.

3 Check the battery negative lead connection to the body or the engine, as applicable. If necessary, unbolt the lead and clean the connector and the area on the body or engine, then bolt the lead into position.

4 If your battery is maintenance-free, there may be a condition indicator fitted to indicate its charge condition. Check your car's handbook, or the battery instructions, for details of how to use the indicator.

5 If your battery isn't maintenance-free, check the electrolyte every few months; this will tell you the battery condition. To do this, you'll need to use a hydrometer – follow the manufacturer's instructions.

Choosing a new battery

As with tyres, it's probably worth phoning around for a few quotes - but make sure you're comparing like with like. The cheapest battery is not necessarily the best buy.

What capacity should the battery have?

Your car's handbook should tell you what "capacity" battery your car needs. This is measured in several ways, but commonly used figures are the "reserve capacity" and the "cold start rating". Generally, the bigger the engine, the higher the battery capacity needs to be.

The reserve capacity rating is how long (in minutes) the battery can supply a current (25 amps) with the engine stopped, under a constant load at 25°C. A typical figure would be 90 minutes.

The cold start rating is the current that the battery will give at –18°C for a specified time. There are different standards for measuring this, and battery manufacturers quote the most favourable one. Typical figures for the same battery would be 200 CCA (Cold Cranking Amps), DIN or 320 CCA, SAE.

Conventional, low-maintenance or maintenance-free?

Most modern cars are fitted with "maintenance-free" batteries when new, and it's best to buy a similar replacement.

"Conventional" batteries need to be checked at regular intervals. This involves checking that the electrolyte is up to the specified level. You may need to top up the battery with distilled water. Plugs are provided in the top of the battery for checking and topping-up.

A "low-maintenance" battery is similar to a conventional battery, but requires less frequent checking.

"Maintenance-free" batteries require no maintenance. They are designed to last for a number of years, and are sometimes fitted with a condition indicator which will show when the battery needs to be recharged or replaced; check the battery instructions for details.

Which size of battery do I need for my car?

There are no standard sizes, so be sure that the new battery will fit in your car. Most battery manufacturers have an applications list to show which batteries fit which cars.

Battery guarantees

Most new batteries are guaranteed to last one or two years for a conventional battery, and four years or more for a maintenance-free battery. Be wary of batteries with no guarantee.

Read the guarantee conditions carefully, and keep the receipt and guarantee card safe.

If you're keeping the car for a few years, it's worth paying the extra for a battery which will last longer.

How to use a battery charger

The battery should not normally need charging from a mains charger, unless it's gone flat, or the car hasn't been used for a long time. If the battery goes flat regularly, it is worth having the electrical system checked by an auto-electrician before buying a new battery, as that may not be the problem (see "Batteries").

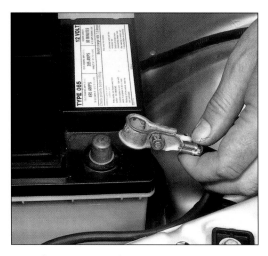

1 Before you start, disconnect the battery leads. If necessary, remove the battery from the car.

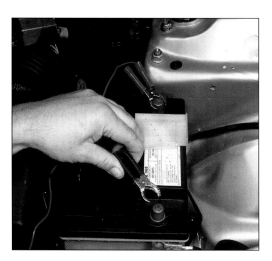

2 Connect the positive (red) charger lead to the battery positive (+) terminal, and the negative (black) lead to the negative (–) terminal.

3 Adjust the charging rate if necessary - see the instructions on the charger (not all can be adjusted.) Plug the battery charger into the mains and switch on.

Buying a battery charger

Make sure that the charger has "thermal overload protection", and "reverse polarity protection".

The "charge rate" determines how quickly a battery can be recharged. The higher the charge rate, the faster a battery can be recharged. There's usually a recommended charge rate marked on the battery, and this rate shouldn't be exceeded.

Some chargers have a "rapid charge" rating, but this can't be used on all batteries (check with the battery manufacturer if in doubt). More expensive chargers have a "boost" setting to start the engine with a flat battery.

Make sure that your charger has a charge indicator, so that you can keep an eye on how far the charging has progressed.

CAUTION

The battery produces flammable gases, so don't smoke or allow any open flames or sparks near the battery. It also contains acid, which will burn if splashed on your skin or in your eyes, and will ruin clothes and paint. When disconnecting the battery always disconnect the earth (negative) lead first, and reconnect it last.

4 When charging is complete, switch off the charger at the mains before disconnecting the leads from the battery. This avoids the danger of sparking at the battery terminals.

When is it charged?

How long the battery takes to charge up depends on how flat it is, what its capacity is and how fast the charger is. See the instructions on the battery charger, or as a rule of thumb, use a rate of 4 to 6 amps overnight.

How to use jump leads

If you have a flat battery, you can start the car by using jump leads to connect its battery temporarily to a charged one, whether in or out of another vehicle.

1 Position the vehicles so that the batteries are close, but don't let the vehicles touch. Switch off the ignition and all electrical equipment on both vehicles, apply the handbrakes, and ensure the gears are in neutral (manual) or "P" (automatic).

2 Connect one end of the RED jump lead to the POSITIVE (+) terminal of the flat battery. Don't let the other end of the red lead touch any vehicle metal.

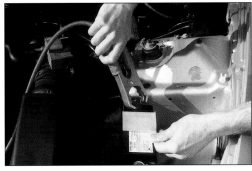

3 Connect the other end of the RED lead to the POSITIVE (+) terminal of the boosting battery.

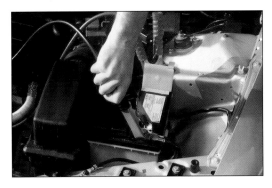

4 Connect one end of the BLACK jump lead to the NEGATIVE (–) terminal of the boosting battery.

5 Connect the other end of the BLACK lead to a bolt or metal bracket, well away from the battery, on the engine block of the vehicle to be started.

6 Ensure that the jump leads cannot come into contact with any moving parts of either engine. Start the engine of the boosting vehicle and run it at a fast idle. Now start the engine of the stranded vehicle and ensure that it's running properly.

7 Stop the engine of the boosting vehicle ONLY, then disconnect the jump leads in the reverse order of connection.

8 Keep the use of electrical equipment to a minimum, and remember that it will take some time for the alternator to charge the battery. Don't stop the engine again too soon – and try not to stall it whilst driving.

Buying jump leads

- Make sure that the leads are thick enough for the job. Some poor-quality leads have very thin wires, and they can melt or catch fire when you use them.
- Make sure that the leads are long enough!
- The leads should be colour coded: red for positive, and black for negative.
- Make sure that the leads have good-quality clamps which will grip securely.
- Are the leads flexible when they're cold? Some go almost rigid and become very difficult to connect.
- Try to buy leads with a case to stop them getting tangled up and keep them in good condition when not being used.

Lights and indicators

When buying a new bulb, you'll need to know what type of fitting (push-fit, bayonet-fit, festoon, etc), and what rating you need.

Ratings are measured in watts (W), and are normally marked on the metal base, or on the glass itself. Some cars have combined tail/stop light bulbs. These bulbs are a bayonet-fit, with offset pins to ensure that the bulb is fitted the correct way round.

The halogen bulbs used in headlights and front foglights have an "H" number to identify their type. It's a good idea to carry a set of spare bulbs in your car, and it's compulsory in some countries.

How to fit a new bulb

Here's a general guide on how to change a halogen-type headlight bulb; you may find differences (for instance access, and bulb type) for your car.

Before you start, make sure that the headlights are switched off. Remember that a bulb that has just failed or been switched off may be extremely hot.

1 Where necessary, unclip the cover from the rear of the headlight for access to the bulb.

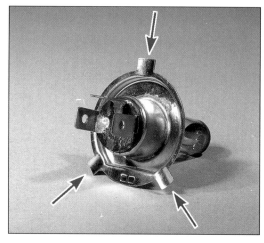

2 Disconnect the wiring plug from the back of the bulb, and pull the rubber cover from the back of the bulb.

3 Release the spring clip, by squeezing its legs together and pulling the clip away from the bulbholder, then pull out the bulb.

4 Don't touch the glass on the new bulb with your fingers – hold it with a tissue or clean cloth. If you accidentally touch the bulb, clean it with a little methylated spirit.

5 Halogen bulbs usually have tangs around their edge so that they only fit in one position. Slide the new bulb into position, then secure it with the spring clip. Refit the bulb cover and reconnect the wiring plug, as applicable.

Faulty lights?

If you find that a light isn't working properly, and the bulb hasn't blown, the most likely cause is a bad electrical connection.

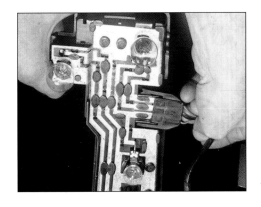
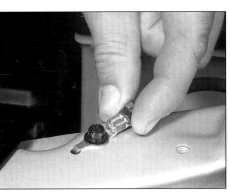

Corrosion

Check the wiring connector(s) for corrosion, and also check the contacts inside the bulbholder. Water may not be able to get in, but condensation can cause trouble.

Clean the affected area, then spray the components with water dispersant. You might have to replace the affected part(s).

Earth connections

If there's no trace of corrosion check the earth connection(s).

Usually the earth wire is bolted to a nearby body panel, or plugged into an earth connector block attached to the body. Check the connections are not corroded, and are tight. If a connection is bolted to a body panel, try cleaning the area of the bodywork with abrasive paper, then reconnect and spray it with water dispersant.

Indicators don't work?

Symptom	Possible cause	Action
Indicators flash faster on one side of the car	• Blown bulb • Incorrect (too low wattage) bulb fitted	• Fit a new bulb • Check the wattage of the bulbs
Indicators flash slower on one side of the car	• Poor earth connection in circuit • Incorrect bulb (too high wattage) bulb fitted	• Refer to "Faulty lights?" • Check the wattage of the bulbs
Indicators come on but don't flash	• Faulty flasher unit • Wiring fault	• Fit a new flasher unit • Have the circuit checked
Indicators don't come on at all	• Blown fuse • Faulty indicator switch • Faulty flasher unit • Wiring fault	• Fit a new fuse • Have the switch tested • Fit a new flasher unit • Have the circuit checked

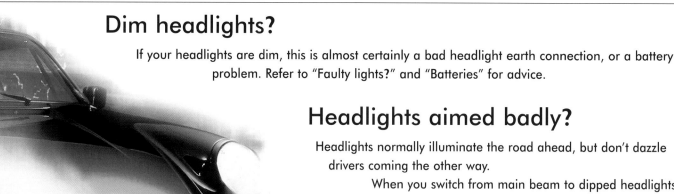

Dim headlights?

If your headlights are dim, this is almost certainly a bad headlight earth connection, or a battery problem. Refer to "Faulty lights?" and "Batteries" for advice.

Headlights aimed badly?

Headlights normally illuminate the road ahead, but don't dazzle drivers coming the other way.

When you switch from main beam to dipped headlights, the beams dip towards the side of the road, away from oncoming traffic.

If you're carrying a load in the back of the car, it will tend to push the back of the car down, which will cause the headlight beams to point higher than usual.

Many cars have a headlight adjuster switch on the dashboard, which can adjust the headlight beams to suit the load being carried. Check your car's handbook for details of the correct settings to use for different loads.

Headlight beam adjustment can only be done accurately by a garage using special equipment.

What to do if a light lens breaks

To protect your car's headlights, you can buy plastic protectors which can be stuck over the lenses.

If you break a lens, tape over the hole temporarily to prevent water getting in.

If the damage is straightforward, and you've kept hold of the broken pieces, you may be able to glue them back in position. Thoroughly clean all the parts first, and make sure you use a suitable type of glue.

If the damage cannot be repaired, you'll have to buy a new part. The lens may be available separately, but often it is an integral part of the light, and you'll have to buy a new light unit. In this case, it may be worth investigating the availability of second-hand parts.

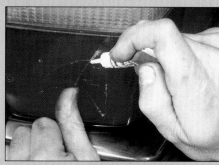

Faulty flasher unit?

If you've got a faulty flasher unit, you need to find out where it is so that you can replace it.

Your car's handbook will have details of where to find the flasher unit, often in the "Fuses and relays" section; it is usually in the main fusebox either behind a cover in the dashboard, or in the engine compartment.

If the flasher unit is working you can find it by switching on the indicators and listening for the clicking noise. Once you get close, you should be able to identify the unit by touching it (you'll be able to feel it clicking).

If you can't locate the flasher unit, ask a garage for advice.

Fuses

Fuses protect a car's electrical circuits from being overloaded. If an electrically-powered item stops working, it could be that the fuse has blown. If you replace a fuse and it blows again, there's almost certainly a fault in the wiring or the item concerned.

Fuses keep blowing

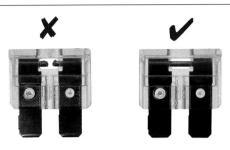

✗   ✔

Fuses are designed to break an electrical circuit when a predetermined current is reached, in order to protect the component(s) and wiring. Any excessive current flow will be due to a fault in the circuit, usually a short-circuit.

A blown fuse can be recognised by the melted wire in the middle.

If a fuse keeps blowing, first of all, check that it's the correct rating for the circuit. Fuse locations and ratings may be marked on the fusebox or the cover, or may be given in your car's handbook. Fuses have standard colour codes. Refer to the markings on the fusebox cover for details of the circuits protected.

If the fuse is of the correct rating, and it still keeps blowing, have the circuit tested for faults.

How to change a fuse

Before you start, switch off the ignition and any other electrical circuits.

1 Check your car's handbook for where to find the fuses. The fuses are usually somewhere under a dashboard cover, but some (or all) might be located under the bonnet.

2 To remove a fuse, simply pull it from its panel. On some cars you'll find a plastic tool for removing the fuses.

3 The new fuse must be the same rating as the old one. It should be the same colour, or have the same number stamped on it.

4 Push the new fuse firmly into its slot in the fusebox. Switch on the circuit concerned. If the new fuse blows, there's a problem.

Warning lights

Your car is fitted with various warning lights to warn you of faults or possible problems with your car's systems. Some warnings are more serious than others, so here's a guide as to what the more common warning lights mean, and what to do if they come on.

Warning light	What does it mean?	What should I do?
Brake fluid level warning*	Low brake fluid level	• Don't drive the car • Check brake fluid level and top up if necessary • Check for brake fluid leaks. If you find a leak, don't drive until the leak has been fixed
Brake pad wear warning*	Brake pads need to be renewed	• The car can be driven • Have the pads renewed as soon as possible
Handbrake "on" warning*	Handbrake is applied	• Check that handbrake is fully released
Charge warning	Alternator is not charging battery	• The car can be driven, but don't drive too far or your battery may go flat • Have the alternator and its wiring checked as soon as possible
Oil pressure warning	Engine oil pressure low	• If light comes on when engine is idling – worn or very hot engine. Check that the light goes out when you "blip" the throttle. • Check the oil level as soon as possible. • If the light comes on when driving – stop the engine immediately, check the oil level and look for oil leaks, then call for assistance if necessary. Serious damage could be caused if you run the engine
Coolant temperature warning	Coolant temperature excessive	• Stop as soon as possible. Allow the engine to cool, then check the coolant level; top up if necessary. • If the light comes on again within a short distance, stop and call for assistance

*NOTE: Sometimes two or more of the brake warning lights are combined. If you suspect that the light may indicate low brake fluid level, DO NOT drive the car until you've checked the level, topped up if necessary, and checked for leaks.

Warning light	What does it mean?	What should I do?
Coolant level warning	Engine coolant level low	• Stop as soon as possible. Allow the engine to cool, then check the coolant level; top up if necessary. • If the light comes on again within a short distance, check for leaks
Engine system warning	Fault code stored in engine management self-diagnostic system	• The car can be driven, but you may notice a loss of performance. Have the engine management system checked as soon as possible
ABS warning	ABS fault	• The car can be driven, but the ABS may not be working (normal braking will not be affected). Have the ABS tested as soon as possible
Airbag (or SRS) warning	Airbag system fault	• The car can be driven, but the airbag system may not work in the event of an accident. Have the airbag system checked as soon as possible
Glow plug warning (diesel)	Glow plugs operating	• Wait for the light to go out before trying to start the engine
Choke warning (petrol)	Choke is applied	• Push the choke control in once the engine has warmed up – the light will then go out
Water in fuel warning (diesel)	Water needs to be drained from the fuel filter	• Refer to "Fluids and filters"
Low fuel warning	Low fuel level in tank	• Fill up soon!

The bodywork and interior

Cleaning your car's bodywork and interior regularly is a good way of preserving its value. Some people swear that their car actually runs better when it's just been washed - that's unlikely to be literally true, but it stands to reason that you'll feel better about driving a sparkling clean vehicle than you will if it's plastered with what is politely known as "road dirt". Your passengers probably prefer to be in clean surroundings too, though anyone who regularly transports small (and not so small) children will know that keeping the car free of sticky debris is a full-time job.

In this chapter we give you some tips on various cleaning and restoration techniques, including how to touch up the inevitable paint chips and minor scars.

How to wash your car

This is the most important thing you can do to protect the paintwork. You'll also spot any stone chips or damage before rust starts to take hold.

Don't use household detergents – they're much too harsh, and they can damage the paint. Don't wash the car in bright sunlight, because the water will dry almost straight away, giving a blotchy finish. Cold water on hot paint can cause tiny cracks in the finish.

1 Rinse the car first using cold water with a bucket and sponge to get rid of dirt and mud, and scrub the wheels. Thick mud can be soaked off using a hose.

Rinse out the bucket, then pour in the recommended amount of soap and fill the bucket with cold water. Don't use too much soap, it will be hard to rinse off and will leave a smeary film.

2 Use a proper car soap or shampoo, which will usually contain wax. This will thoroughly clean the paintwork, and you'll end up with a nice shiny finish.

3 Soap the car using a soft, clean sponge, then rinse with cold water. Dry off using a chamois leather, which will absorb the water, and give a shiny finish without streaks.

129

How to polish your car

If you find that the water no longer "beads" on your car's paintwork when it rains, or when you wash it, a coat of polish wouldn't hurt!

Most modern polishes use wax and/or silicone, and these clean the paintwork, and leave a layer of protective wax on top. Read the label to make sure that the polish is suitable for your car – for example, some polishes can't be used on metallic paintwork. Many paint finishes use two coats, a base colour coat, with a clear coat of resin over the top - don't use abrasive polishes on these finishes, or you'll remove the clear coat.

Don't polish in strong sunlight. If you do, the polish will dry immediately, and it will be hard to remove (you may even end up scratching the paint trying to get the polish off).

Before you start, wash the car, and thoroughly dry it.

You'll need two soft cloths: one for applying the polish, and one for buffing-off. Cotton cloths are best to avoid the problem of bits of cloth sticking to the paint as you polish.

It's best to work on one panel at a time – if you try to put polish on the whole car, then buff it off, the polish you put on first will have dried by the time you come to buff it off.

Apply a light even layer of polish, using a light circular motion, then let it dry to a haze (not a white powder), and lightly buff it off using your buffing cloth.

If you get polish on the glass, rub it off straight away unless the label says it's suitable for glass – most polishes aren't.

If the polish gets onto plastic trim panels, it can discolour them when it dries. You can get rid of these marks using a grease or wax remover (available from most car accessory shops), but read the label to make sure that it's suitable, and follow the instructions.

You can restore the look of plastic trim parts using a plastic cleaner or colour restorer (again, read the instructions). These can work wonders with faded plastic, but make sure you wipe any overspill off the paintwork straight away.

Matt paint?

As your car gets older, the paintwork might start to fade, looking dull and dirty even after you've washed it.

As long as things haven't got too bad, you should be able to revive the paint using a colour restorer. You can buy a whole range of restorers: some are more abrasive than others, some are especially for metallic paint, and some are coloured for use on a certain paint colour. All these products work by removing a layer of paint, so take care!

It's best to start off with a restorer which is only mildly abrasive. Paint is easy to take off, but you can't put it back on! Try it out on a small area first to see what the results will be before you start on a large panel – don't rub too hard, some remove paint very quickly.

You'll need plenty of soft cloths. Use separate cloths for applying the colour restorer, and for buffing-off. Changing the cloths as they become covered with paint. Cotton cloths are best to avoid the problem of bits of cloth sticking to the paint as you work.

Once you're satisfied with the results, apply a coat of polish.

How to touch-up paint chips and scratches

Use the wire brush supplied with the touch-up stick, or a small piece of fine wire wool, to remove any rust. Try not to damage the good paintwork around the scratch (wrapping wire wool around the end of a pencil helps).

Next, clean around the scratch. It's best to use plain water, anything else might damage the paintwork, or stop the new paint sticking. Let the paintwork dry fully.

The paint must be thoroughly mixed, usually by shaking the touch-up stick for a few minutes; follow the instructions. Apply a small amount of paint, using the touch-up stick brush or, better still, a very fine artist's brush. Work slowly, and brush one way. Try to "fill" the scratch – don't let the new paint build up higher than the good paint around the scratch. With a two-coat finish, follow the instructions and apply the clear coat after the colour coat has dried properly.

Wait a few days for the paint to dry properly, then rub the painted area using a polishing compound (or a very mild abrasive colour restorer) to blend in the new paint. Once you're happy with the result, wash and polish the car to finish off.

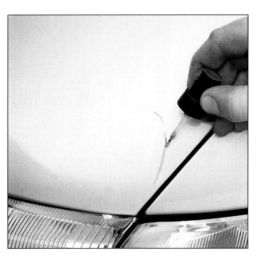
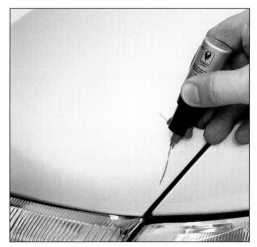
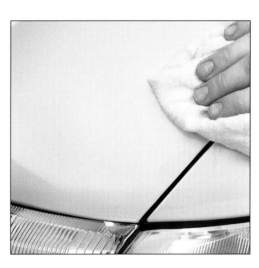

Choosing the right touch-up paint

Every car has a paint code, which is usually stamped onto a metal plate when the car is painted at the factory. If you're going to buy paint from an official parts dealer, take your car along – the staff will know where to find the code, often on a plate under the bonnet.

Car accessory shops also sell touch-up paint; all you need to know is the manufacturer's name for the paint colour, and when the car was built. Although these paints are usually a close match to the original, they're rarely exact matches. If you want to be sure of an exact colour match, you should always buy the paint from a dealer for your make of car.

You can usually buy touch-up paint in two forms: the easy-to-use "touch-up stick", or a spray-can. The stick consists of a small canister of paint, with a brush built into the lid. Sometimes you'll also get a wire brush for removing rust and flaky paint from the scratch, but take care if you decide to use it – the sharp bristles can make a mess of perfectly good paint.

Rust

If you've got major rust problems, you'll need the help of a bodywork expert, but small rust spots are quite easy to fix.

If you notice a rust spot when you're cleaning the car, it's best to get rid of it as soon as you can, before it develops into a more serious problem.

There are many rust treatment kits available from car accessory shops; follow the instructions.

Fixing loose trim

If you find that a piece of trim is loose, it's worth taking the time to fix it before it falls off. Most trim parts are held on with clips or strong adhesive tape. Never try to glue it back into position – the repair probably won't last long, and you may damage the paintwork.

Trim panels secured by adhesive tape

You can buy special trim tape from car accessory shops. In many cases, it's best to pull the trim right off, and reattach it using new tape. Once you've removed the trim, you need to clean off all the old adhesive; it can be difficult, so you might need to buy adhesive remover (follow the instructions supplied).

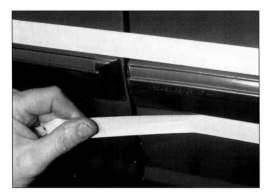

1 To line up the trim when you refit it, you can stick masking tape along the body. Align it with other trim strips, or measure from the edge of the panel to make sure it's straight.

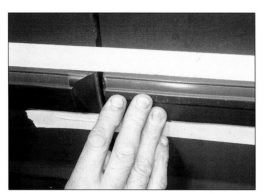

2 Cut the adhesive tape as necessary, and stick it to the back of the trim or the bodywork. On wide trim strips, you'll have to use two strips of tape side-by-side. Hold the trim in position, and check that the tape is thick enough to stick the trim to the body. Sometimes you'll need a double thickness of tape.

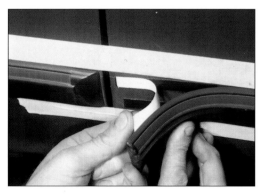

3 Remove the backing paper and, working from one end, push the trim firmly into position, lining it up with the masking tape.

Trim panels secured by clips

If you find that a clip's broken, you might have to release the surrounding clips to pull the trim away to fit the new clip. Take care, it's very easy to break more clips.

You should be able to buy new clips from your local parts dealer. Make sure that you get the correct clip.

Fit the new clip, then fit the panel back into position

Squeaky doors

A squeaky door is almost bound to be dry hinges. This is fixed by opening the door, and oiling or greasing the hinges, using a multi-purpose grease. An aerosol lubricant will usually work wonders too. Once you've applied the grease or spray, open and close the door a few times to work the lubricant into the hinges. Wipe off any excess grease or spray to stop it finding its way onto the bodywork and trim, and your clothes.

Interior

A regular clearout and clean-up is easier than an annual blitz and will keep your car looking good. Try to pick a fine day as you'll need to have the doors open. You will need a vacuum cleaner, duster/polishing cloths and spray-on cleaner (various types of spray-on cleaner are available from car accessory shops - choose whatever suits your needs).

First of all, take out all the loose items you've been carrying around. Remove the floor mats, if fitted, empty the ashtrays, and pull out the stereo unit if it's the removable kind.

Open all the doors wide, and vacuum up any loose dirt, grit, etc. Don't forget to vacuum in between and underneath the front seats. Try to use a separate brush attachment for the seats. While you're using the vacuum cleaner, carry on and clean the boot. If your car has folding rear seats, lift the cushion(s) and clean underneath.

Inspect the carpets, if you find any stains, use a spray-on cleaner, working it in with a nail-brush and vacuuming or sponging off, according to the instructions. You'll probably find the worst ground-in dirt on the driver's side carpet, especially near the pedals.

Check seats for marks and use fabric cleaner to deal with these.

Allow any dampened seats and carpets to dry before using the car. If you have access to a suitable wet-and-dry vacuum cleaner, this can be used to speed up the drying.

Now that the dust-raising is over, you can finish off with the interior trim. Use a soft duster to remove the surface dust before cleaning with a suitable trim cleaner. As well as removing grime, these normally help to keep the car smelling fresh.

Windows are best cleaned using a chamois leather, but difficult marks can be removed with a glass cleaner, buffing finally with a soft cloth.

Getting rid of smells

If the problem is due to spillage, you'll need to clean the affected area using a suitable cleaner – see "Interior ". Depending on the type of spillage, you may need to clean the affected area with disinfectant first, but read the instructions on the label to make sure that it won't damage the relevant trim.

Once you've got rid of the source of trouble, you may still be left with an unpleasant smell. Parking the car with the windows open should help to reduce the problem.

Most car accessory shops sell a range of air fresheners for cars. You should be able to buy one with "odour-neutralising" properties which will help to get rid of any lingering smells. Read the the packaging to decide which product is the best for your needs.

Cleaning plastic trim parts

Use a suitable plastic cleaner, which you can buy from car accessory shops. Read the instructions on the label when you're choosing a cleaner, because not all cleaners are suitable for all plastics.

When using cleaners or restorers on the plastic trim panels, it's best to apply the cleaner or restorer to a clean cloth, then use the cloth to rub it onto the plastic, this will help to avoid getting plastic cleaner or restorer on the paintwork. Wipe any overspill off the paintwork straight.

Where do I go for help?

This chapter gives some hints on choosing a garage and on communicating your requirements. If you can explain clearly what your problem is or what work you expect to have done, there's less chance of an unpleasant surprise when you receive the bill. There's also some information on warranties, pointers to the best places to buy consumables such as tyres and exhaust systems, advice on buying and selling cars and tips on how to save money on insurance.

Choosing a garage

If you need to have work done on your car, whether it's servicing, repair work, or fitting extras, how do you decide where to take it? You may decide to carry out the work yourself, or you may have a suitably-qualified friend who's willing to help; otherwise you'll need to find a garage to do the work for you.

If your car is still under warranty, always take it to an authorised dealer for any work or checks to be carried out; if you take it anywhere else, you may invalidate the warranty.

If you want to ensure that your car has an authentic service history when you come to sell it, then you may decide to have all work done by an authorised dealer. Generally, this will be the most expensive option, but you'll have the satisfaction of knowing that genuine manufacturer's procedures and parts will be used for all the work.

If your car needs tyres, exhaust parts, shock absorbers, or even a new clutch, it's worth trying one of the specialist fitting centres. Many will offer you an all-inclusive price for a particular job, often with a comprehensive warranty, and for far less than a garage.

If you're not prepared to pay the rates charged by an authorised dealer, you may decide to take your car to one of the smaller independent garages. Some specialise in a particular make of car and, although they may not be authorised dealers, you'll often find that their expertise is equal to that of the manufacturer's trained personnel. If you're going to take your car to an independent garage, it's always worth visiting several in your area, and asking them for a price for the work to be carried out. Always ask for a written firm price, and check to see what's included (see "How much will it cost?").

Does the garage have a good reputation?

Pay a visit to the garage, and talk to one of the mechanics to get a feel for the enthusiasm and knowledge of the staff, and the standard of service. There's no reason to treat small garages with suspicion, many provide a better service than authorised dealers, but unfortunately there are still a few rogues around who will take advantage of the unwary.

At a smaller garage, you can't always expect the "fancy" service provided by a larger dealer; there may not be a carpeted waiting area, and you may not be provided with a courtesy car, but remember that a dealer is building these "perks" into your bill.

Ask around to see if anyone you know has had good or bad experience of dealing with any of the garages you're thinking of using. Reputation is very important, and it's often better to pay a little extra to take your car to a garage with a known good reputation.

Explaining a problem

If you've got a problem with your car, how do you explain it to the service manager or mechanic at the local garage? Remember that most garages will charge you at an hourly rate, so any extra information is likely to save you money in the long run.

If you haven't been able to identify a problem, here are a few things which you're likely to be asked when you take your car to the garage.

◆ Does the problem occur all the time, or is it intermittent?
◆ Does the problem occur when the engine's cold, hot or both?
◆ Are there any other symptoms (noises, vibration, etc)?
◆ Has the car been regularly serviced?
◆ Have you had any work carried out on the car recently?

If the problem occurs all the time, the best thing is to take the mechanic out for a drive and demonstrate it.

Intermittent problems can be difficult to trace and cure. If the problem is present for a while before disappearing, take the car to the garage when the problem is present. Most mechanical problems will be relatively easy to trace, but engine problems can be tricky. Sometimes the garage may have no option but to renew various components until the problem disappears – this could prove to be expensive.

Always ask for a written firm price (sometimes it may not be possible to give an accurate final price), otherwise you may be faced with a large unexpected bill.

What's included?

The items on a garage bill usually fall into one of three categories: parts, labour and consumables. Parts include any new parts which may be required during the work. Labour covers the cost of the time taken (in hours) by the mechanic to carry out the work. Consumables cover items such oil, coolant, cleaning fluids, etc.

Always ask for an itemised list so that you can see exactly what's been included.

Here are a few things which you should ask when getting a price for a job:

◆ What's the hourly labour rate?
◆ How long should the work take?
◆ Will genuine or pattern parts be used?
◆ Is VAT included?
◆ Will the work be covered by a warranty? (Ask for details of the warranty)

Comparing rough prices for work

Be sure that you're making a fair comparison, as the prices may be structured differently.

You can check the cost of genuine parts by asking at an authorised dealer, or of pattern parts from a motor factor. A garage will almost certainly pay a "trade" price for parts which will always be less than the "retail" price.

If you're having any new parts fitted, check whether the work will be covered by a parts and labour warranty; if not, ask why.

You should find that the prices are similar and, by comparing them, you'll be able to spot any discrepancies or suspicious costs. Ask if there's anything you don't understand.

Once you decide to have the work done, ask the garage to contact you immediately if they encounter any problems which will involve additional work.

If you don't do this, many will carry out the work anyway, and charge you accordingly.

How much will it cost?

Whenever you're intending to get any work done, get a written firm price before you agree. It's always wise to get rough prices from several different garages so that you can compare them. Beware of verbal prices, particularly over the telephone; if your bill turns out to be more than expected, you won't have a case to argue unless you have a written firm price.

Checking the bill

Always ask for an itemised bill, which will give you a full breakdown of all the costs, and will allow you to see exactly what work has been carried out.

◆ Check the details of the bill against the firm price, and query any discrepancies. If you find that "miscellaneous" costs appear on your bill, ask what they are.

◆ Check the labour costs against the garage's quoted hourly rate, and check the price of any parts used (see "What's included?").

◆ Check that the work described on the bill has been carried out (see "Checking the work"), and if there's any evidence that you've been billed for work which hasn't been done, query it with the mechanic concerned.

Once you've checked the bill, and you're happy that it's accurate, it's time to dip into your bank account!

Understanding the mechanic

When you're talking about any work to be done on your car, don't let yourself be baffled. "Glossary" should help you to understand the terminology used, and the explanations of how systems work should be useful too. Make sure that you understand what work the garage is intending to do. Ask if there may be any problems; for instance, there can be seized or broken fasteners to contend with, which may make the job more difficult.

Sometimes, a mechanic may point out other potential problems whilst carrying out work on your car. The mechanic might suggest that you'll need a set of brake discs and pads soon. Always check this for yourself, or ask the mechanic to show you the problem. If in doubt, ask for a second opinion from an experienced friend or another garage.

Checking the work

If components have been renewed, many garages leave the old components in a box in the boot so that you can see that the work has been carried out, and was necessary. It's a good idea to ask the mechanic to do this when you take your car in for work to be done.

If your car has been serviced, check that a new (clean) oil filter has been fitted, and pull out the dipstick to check for fresh oil. You should be able to tell where work has been done, because the area around the work should be cleaner than the rest of the car.

If the work involved disturbing any gaskets or seals, park the car overnight with a sheet of card or paper underneath (or pick a clean piece of road or driveway) so that you can check for signs of leaks in the morning. If you notice any leaks, take the car back to have them fixed, and don't let the garage charge you for fixing the problem (unless it's totally unrelated to the work they've done).

If the work involved removing the wheels, it's a good idea to check that you can remove the wheel nuts or bolts to change a wheel (see "Removing a wheel").

Warranties

Whenever you buy a new or second-hand car, a warranty should be included. Similarly, when you have any work carried out, the work should be covered by a warranty.

The warranties provided with new cars are normally very comprehensive, and often include membership of one of the breakdown organisations. You may be offered the chance to take out an "extended warranty" on a new car. Always check carefully what's covered by an extended warranty (is there a claim limit, and is anything excluded?), and weigh this up against the cost. An extended warranty can be a very expensive way of buying peace-of-mind, especially if it ties you to having the car serviced by the dealer.

When buying a second-hand car, always check what sort of warranty you're getting. You'll generally find that there's a maximum claim limit, which is often so low that it effectively limits claims to very minor problems. If you have to pay extra for a warranty, read the small-print very carefully – you'll probably find that it's not worth the extra cost.

If you have any work done which involves the fitting of new components (especially major items such as an engine or gearbox), make sure that the work is covered by a parts and labour warranty. This will cover you against the use of any faulty parts, and any mistakes made by the mechanic which might cause trouble later. Check that the bill states the work is covered by a warranty, and be sure the warranty period is specified.

Buying parts

To be sure of obtaining the correct parts, you'll need to know the model and year of manufacture of your car, and it will sometimes be necessary to quote the Vehicle Identification Number (VIN). Your car's handbook will usually show you where to find the VIN. It can also be useful to take the old parts along for identification. Parts such as starter motors and alternators may be available under a service exchange.

Accessory shops

These are good for components needed for car maintenance. Items of this sort from a reputable shop are usually of the same standard as those used by the car manufacturer.

Besides components, these shops also sell tools and general accessories, have convenient opening hours and charge lower prices. Some accessory shops have parts counters where components needed for almost any repair job can be bought or ordered.

Motor factors

Good factors will stock all the more important components which wear out comparatively quickly, and can supply individual parts needed for the overhaul of a larger assembly (eg, brake seals and hydraulic parts, engine bearing shells, pistons, valves, etc).

Tyre and exhaust specialists

These may be independent, or members of a chain. They frequently offer competitive prices when compared with a dealer or local garage. When researching prices, also ask what "extras" may be added - fitting a valve and wheel balancing are often both charged on top of the price of a new tyre.

Other sources

Beware of parts or materials bought from market stalls, car boot sales, etc. These items aren't necessarily sub-standard, but there's little chance of compensation if they are unsatisfactory. In the case of safety-critical components such as brake pads, there's also the risk of a failure causing injury or death.

Second-hand components obtained from a car breaker can be a good buy in some circumstances, but this sort of purchase is best made by an experienced DIY mechanic.

Officially appointed garages

This is the best source for parts which are peculiar to your car (eg, badges, interior trim, body panels, etc). It's the only place you should buy parts if your car is still under warranty.

Selling a car

If you're going to sell your car, the first thing to do is to decide what price to ask. There are car price guides available from newsagents. The price you can expect depends on the car's age, condition and mileage. Don't ask too much, but it may be a good idea to ask for more than you're prepared to accept, then there's some room for negotiation between you and the buyer.

Once you're decided on how much to ask for your car, you need to advertise it. Local papers and magazines carry advertisements for a reasonable cost. If you want to reach a more specific audience, place an advert in one of the specialist car sales papers or magazines.

Think about the wording of your advert. You need to give as much positive information as possible, without using too many words. Give details of the model and engine size, service history (where applicable), colour, age, mileage, condition and any desirable options or equipment. If you've owned the car from new, it's always worth stating "one owner".

Bear in mind the points which the prospective buyer should be looking for, as described in "Buying second-hand". It goes without saying that the car should be clean and tidy, as first impressions are important. Any fluid leaks should be cured, and there's no point in trying to disguise any major bodywork or mechanical problems.

Make sure that the service documents, registration document, etc, are available for inspection. If the old test certificate has only a few months to run, get a new one if you can do so without too much expense - it will make the car much more saleable.

You're likely to sell your car more quickly and get a better price if you sell at the right time of year. It's always best to sell in the spring or summer rather than in the winter.

If you're trading the car in with a dealer, you will probably get a lower price than if you sell privately. If selling privately, don't allow the buyer to take the car away until you have their money, and it's a good idea to ask them to sign a piece of paper to say that they're happy to buy the car as viewed, just in case any problems develop later on. Give a receipt for the money paid.

Buying new

This is the most expensive option, but also the most secure - you are protected against anything going wrong with the car.

Find your dealer
Look in Yellow Pages to identify the local dealers who sell the make of car you want. If there's more than one, it's well worth contacting all of them – just because they sell the same cars, it doesn't mean that they will offer you the same deal!

What's included?
When you've driven the car, and decided on the specification and colour that suits you, check on what will be included in the price (are number plates, road tax and delivery charges included?). Most new cars are sold with a comprehensive warranty package, which will often include breakdown insurance.

Start haggling!
Unless you're buying a particularly sought-after model, the manufacturer's list price is the absolute maximum which you should pay, and there's always scope for the dealer to offer a discount. You'll almost certainly get a better deal at a time of year when the dealer isn't selling many cars, for instance around Christmas.

Buying second-hand

The safest way is to buy from a recognised dealer. Riskier alternatives are to buy at auction (not recommended for the average buyer) or privately. If you can't afford to have the car inspected professionally, take a knowledgeable friend with you, and bear in mind the following points.

◆ **Don't buy the first car to catch your attention.** If you've never driven the model of car you're thinking of buying, it's a good idea to view and drive several examples so that you can compare them.

◆ **If you're buying privately, ask to see the service receipts and test certificates.** This will help to establish that the car hasn't been stolen, and that the recorded mileage is genuine. Always ask to view the car at the seller's private address, to make sure that it isn't being sold by an unscrupulous dealer posing as a private seller.

◆ **Don't be put off by high mileage.** Most modern cars are capable of completing 100,000 miles or more without major problems, provided that they have been well-maintained. A high mileage car which has been used mainly for motorway cruising may be in better shape than a low-mileage car which has been used for short journeys.

◆ **Check the service history.** The service book supplied with the car when new should have been completed and stamped by an authorised garage after each service. Cars with a full service history ("fsh") usually command a higher price than those without. If the car is 3 years old or more, check that it has a new or very recent MoT certificate.

◆ **Don't view in the dark or wet.** Water on the bodywork can give a misleading impression of the condition of the paintwork.

◆ **Check the indicated mileage, and ask yourself if it's genuine.** If the car has covered a high mileage, there will often be signs of wear on the driver's seat, in the driver's footwell around the pedals and on the pedal rubbers.

◆ **Check for rust, and for signs of new or mis-matched paint, which might show that the car has been involved in an accident.** Check the tyres for signs of unusual wear or damage, and check that the car "sits" evenly on its suspension, with all four corners at the same height.

◆ **Open the bonnet.** Check for any obvious fluid leakage (oil, water, brake fluid), then start the engine and listen for any unusual noises. Also check for signs of excessive exhaust smoke. Blue smoke often indicates worn engine components, which may prove expensive to repair.

◆ **Check the locks.** One key should operate all the locks and the ignition switch – if not, it's likely that the car has been broken into at some stage, and one or more of the locks has been replaced.

◆ **Drive the car, and test the brakes, steering and gearbox.** Make sure that the car doesn't pull to one side, and check that the steering feels positive and that the gears can be selected satisfactorily. Listen for any unusual noises or vibration, and keep an eye on the instruments and warning lights to make sure that they're working.

◆ **Don't be rushed into a deal.** There are plenty more cars to look at.

Check this out!

There are several organisations which, for a small fee, will carry out checks on a car to ensure that there's no outstanding finance owed by a previous owner, and that the car has not been declared an insurance write-off. If money is owed to a finance company, the car could be repossessed, and you may have no right to compensation! The same applies if you inadvertently buy a stolen car.

Second-hand woes

Many dealers offer comprehensive warranties, but beware of some of the warranty plans sold with second-hand cars. You'll often find that there's a maximum claim limit, which may be so low that it limits the warranty to very minor problems. Items such as clutch and brake linings, drivebelts and cooling system hoses - the components most likely to cause problems on an older car - will almost certainly be excluded. If it's suggested that you pay extra for a warranty, read the small print carefully – you'll probably find that it's not worth the extra.

Car insurance

It's always worth shopping around for insurance quotes, because they can vary enormously. Insurance is big business, and there are specialist companies who offer good rates to drivers above a certain age, drivers with a poor driving record, etc.

The best way to save money is to keep your driving record clean, and shop around when the insurance is due for renewal, but there are other steps to reduce the bill.

What type of cover should I choose?

Fully comprehensive cover will provide you with full cover for any damage to your car, even if you back into a gate post. Third party, fire and theft (TPFT) cover will provide you with cover against damaging other people's cars or property, and will also cover your car if it catches fire, or is stolen. TPFT cover will not, however, cover you if you accidentally damage your own car. The remaining option is "third party only" (TP) cover, which is really only worth considering if you have a very cheap car. It will only cover you for damage to other people's cars and property, and you won't be covered if your car is stolen or catches fire. Fully comprehensive insurance costs more than other types of insurance, but bear in mind that the cost of repairing accident damage on a modern car can be very high.

Although your policy will usually give you cover to meet the minimum requirements in Europe, you may have to pay an additional premium if you want the same level of cover which you have at home.

What information will the insurance company need?

Make sure that you provide accurate information, and answer any questions honestly. If you give any false information, or "forget" to mention anything important, your insurance is likely to be invalid, and you could be in serious trouble if you have an accident.

Although some insurance companies may ask for additional information, most of them will ask for the information in the following list:

◆ Your name, address and postcode
◆ The names of any other drivers who will drive the car
◆ The dates of birth of all drivers including yourself
◆ The occupations of all drivers including yourself
◆ Details of any accidents you or any of the drivers has had in the last few years
◆ Details of any recent motoring offences or convictions for any of the drivers
◆ The make, model and registration number of the car
◆ The car's current value
◆ Details of any modifications from the car's standard specification
◆ Whether you'll be using the car in connection with your work
◆ Where you'll be parking the car overnight (garage, driveway or street)
◆ What sort of cover you require

How can I reduce the premium?

Insurance costs are higher for young and/or inexperienced drivers, so by restricting the cover to only older experienced drivers to drive the car, the insurance premium will be reduced. If your car doesn't cover very many miles, you can reduce your premium by restricting the annual mileage. In some cases, you can make a saving on your premium by adding a voluntary excess to your policy, although you'll have to pay a higher contribution towards any claim.

No-claim bonus

Every year that you are insured without making a claim, your insurer gives you a discount, up to a maximum of 60% or 65% after 5 or 6 years. If you make a claim, you lose one or two years' worth of discount - so think about whether it's worth putting in a claim to cover the cost of repairing minor damage, especially if you have to pay an excess.

Some companies offer "no-claims protection" for an extra fee. Read the small print carefully before deciding whether this extra insurance is worthwhile.

Comparing quotes

Many policies provide windscreen cover without affecting your no-claims bonus, and you may have the use of a courtesy car whilst your own is being repaired. Many of the larger insurance companies deal with their own approved repairers, so if you need to have damage repaired, you won't have to take your car to several different garages for repair prices. You may also find that the insurance company will arrange for your car to be picked up and delivered back to you when the repairs are complete. When you're comparing insurance quotes, make sure that you're comparing similar packages.

You may be asked if you want "legal protection"; sometimes this is included automatically with your policy. This service is worth having, as it will help to recover any costs which you may have to pay in the case of an accident which wasn't your fault.

Making a claim

Read your policy document so that you know what to do if you have to make a claim.

If you have to make an insurance claim, inform your insurance company as soon as possible. You'll have to fill in a claim form, giving details of exactly what happened. Make sure that you give as much information as possible, and if you're involved in an accident, try to obtain the name and address of an independent witness.

Breakdown organisations

A breakdown can prove to be expensive if you find yourself stranded at the roadside. Garage recovery charges can be very high, especially if you suffer a breakdown on a motorway. If you have to call out a recovery vehicle, you'll almost certainly find that the call-out charge will be more than the cost of a year's membership of one of the breakdown organisations. If you're not a member of a breakdown organisation, a local garage will usually only recover your car to their premises, in which case you'll still have to pay to get your car fixed. If your car can't be fixed quickly, you'll be stranded without transport.

You'll find that there are a number of packages available from the various motoring organisations, and you should be able to find one that suits your requirements. Some will guarantee to take your car and passengers to your home or to your destination, whichever suits you best, whilst others may only transport your car to the nearest garage. You may also be able to choose an option which will provide assistance if you have trouble starting your car at home, and some packages will provide full cover if you take your car abroad.

Obtain information from several breakdown organisations, and read everything carefully before deciding which package is most suitable. Always check carefully to see what's included, and make sure you're aware of any limits on the cover.

Glossary

The following information isn't intended to be an Automotive waffle-to-English dictionary, but it should help you to understand some of the more common terms which you'll come across when discussing your car with your local garage, or when talking to the local pub-bore!

ABS – Anti-lock Braking System. Uses sensors at each wheel to sense when the wheels are about to lock, and releases the brakes to prevent locking. Refer to "Running gear".

Air bag – An inflatable bag which inflates in the event of a head-on collision to protect the driver and/or front passenger from injury. Driver's air bags are usually mounted in the steering wheel and passenger's airbags are usually mounted in the dashboard. Refer to "Safety".

Air conditioning – A system which enables the temperature of the air inside the car to be lowered, and dehumidifies the air. This allows more comfort and rapid demisting. Refer to "Cooling and heating".

Air filter – A renewable paper or foam filter which removes foreign particles from the air which is sucked into the engine. Refer to "Fluids and filters".

Airflow sensor – A sensor used in an engine management system to measure the amount of air being sucked into the engine. Refer to "The engine".

Alternator – An electrical generator which is driven by the engine. Its job is to provide electricity for the car's electrical system when the engine's running, and to charge the battery. Refer to "Electrical things".

Antifreeze – A fluid which is added to water to produce coolant. The antifreeze stops the coolant freezing in cold weather, and prevents corrosion inside the engine. Refer to "Cooling and heating".

Anti-roll bar – A metal bar used in front and/or rear suspension systems to reduce the tendency of the car's body to roll from side-to-side. Not all cars have anti-roll bars. Refer to "Running gear".

Anti-seize compound – a grease coating which reduces the chances of seizing on components subjected to high temperatures and pressures.

Axle – A spindle on which a wheel revolves.

Ball bearing – A bearing consisting of two hardened metal rings, with hardened steel balls between them

Balljoint – A maintenance-free flexible joint used mainly in suspension and steering systems to allow for movement of the components. Consists of a metal ball and cup, with a rubber seal to retain the grease.

Battery – A "reservoir" which stores electricity. Provides the power to start the engine, and power for the electrical systems when the engine's stopped, and is charged by the alternator when the engine's running. Refer to "Electrical things".

Bearing – A metal or other hard-wearing surface against which another part moves, and which is designed to reduce friction and wear. A bearing is usually lubricated.

Big-end – The lower end of a connecting rod which is attached to the crankshaft. It incorporates a bearing, and transmits the movement of the connecting rod to the crankshaft. Refer to "The engine".

Bleed nipple (or valve) – A screw, usually hollow, which allows fluid or air to be bled out of a system when it's loosened.

Bore – A term used to describe the diameter of a cylinder in an engine. Refer to "The engine".

Brake backplate – A metal plate bolted to the rear suspension, which carries the rear drum brake components. Refer to "Running gear".

Brake bleeding – A procedure for removing air from the brake hydraulic system.

Brake caliper – The part of a disc brake system which houses the brake pads and the hydraulic pistons. The caliper straddles the brake disc, and is mounted on a fixed part of the suspension. Refer to "Running gear".

Brake disc – A rotating metal disc coupled to a roadwheel, which is clamped between two brake pads in a disc brake system. As the brake disc slows down due to friction, so does the roadwheel. Refer to "Running gear".

Brake drum – A rotating metal drum coupled to a roadwheel. The brake shoes rub on the inside of the drum. As the brake drum slows down due to friction, so does the roadwheel. Refer to "Running gear".

Brake fade – A temporary reduction in braking power due to overheating of the brake friction material.

Brake fluid – A hydraulic fluid resistant to high temperatures, used in hydraulic braking systems, and some hydraulic clutch systems. Refer to "Fluids and filters".

Brake pad – A metal plate, with a pad of hard-wearing friction material bonded to one side. When the brakes are applied, the hydraulic pistons in the brake caliper push the pads against the brake disc. Refer to "Running gear".

Brake servo – A vacuum-operated device which increases the effort applied by the brake pedal to the brake master cylinder. Vacuum is supplied from the inlet manifold on a petrol engine, or from a vacuum pump on a diesel engine. Refer to "Running gear".

Brake shoe – A curved metal former with friction material bonded to the outside surface. When the brake are applied, the hydraulic pistons in the wheel cylinder push the brake shoes against the brake drum. Refer to "Running gear".

Breather – An opening or valve which allows air or fumes out of a system, or fresh air into a system.

Bucket tappet – A bucket-shaped cam follower usually fitted to the top of a valve.

Bump stop – A hard piece of rubber or plastic used in many suspension systems to prevent the moving parts from touching the body during violent suspension movements.

Caliper – See Brake caliper.

Cam belt – See Timing belt.

Camber angle – The angle at which the wheels are set from the vertical when viewed from the front of the car. Negative camber is when the wheels tilt inwards at the top.

Cam follower (tappet) – A component used to transfer the rotary movement of the camshaft lobes to the up-and-down movement required to operate the valves.

Camshaft – A rotating shaft driven from the crankshaft, with lobes or cams used to operate the valves, via the valve gear. Refer to "The engine".

Camshaft lobes – Eccentric sections on the camshaft used to operate the valves via the valve gear.

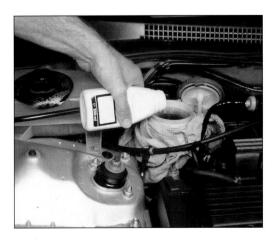

Camshaft sensor - A sensor used in an engine management system to provide information on the position of the camshaft.

Carburettor – A device which is used to mix air and petrol in the correct proportions required for burning by the engine. Superseded on modern cars by fuel injection systems.

Castor angle – the angle between a front wheel's steering pivot axis and a vertical line through the centre of the wheel.

Catalytic converter – A device built fitted in the exhaust system which reduces the amount of harmful gases released into the atmosphere. Refer to "The engine".

Choke – Either the device which reduces the amount of air entering a carburettor during cold starting (in order to provide extra petrol), or a term to describe the passage where the throttle valve is located in a carburettor.

Centrifugal advance – System for controlling the ignition timing using weights rotating on a shaft in the distributor to alter the ignition timing according to engine speed.

Circlip – A ring-shaped sprung steel clip which locates in a groove to prevent endwise movement of cylindrical parts and shafts.

Closed loop – A term for an emission control system using a catalytic converter where the engine management system controls the air/fuel mixture to allow the catalytic converter to operate at maximum efficiency. Refer to "The engine".

Clutch – A friction device which allows two rotating components to be coupled together smoothly, without the need for either rotating component to stop moving. Refer to "The transmission".

Coil – See Ignition coil.

Coil spring – A spiral coil of sprung steel used in many suspension systems. Refer to "Running gear".

Combustion chamber – Shaped area into which the air/fuel mixture is compressed by the piston, and where the mixture is ignited. The combustion chamber may be formed in the cylinder head, or sometimes in the top of the piston. Refer to "The engine".

Compression ratio (CR) – A term to describe the amount by which the air/fuel mixture is compressed as a piston moves from the bottom to the top of its travel. 10.0:1 CR means that the volume of mixture at the top of the piston travel is one tenth of the volume at the bottom of the piston travel.

Condenser – Either a device which prevents excessive sparking at the contact breaker points, or a component in an air conditioning system which condenses gaseous refrigerant into a liquid.

Connecting rod (con rod) – A metal rod in the engine connecting a piston to the crankshaft. The connecting rod transfers the up-and-down motion of the piston to the crankshaft. Refer to "The engine".

Constant velocity (CV) joint – A joint used in driveshafts, where the speed of the input shaft is exactly the same as the speed of the output shaft no matter what the angle of the joint. Refer to "The transmission".

Contact breaker (points) – A device used in the distributor on older cars. Two electrical contacts (points) open and close via a cam to switch the ignition HT circuit on and off, providing sparks at the spark plugs.

Coolant – A liquid consisting of a mixture of water and antifreeze, used in a car's engine cooling system. Refer to "Cooling and heating".

Coolant (water) pump – A pump driven by the engine which pumps the coolant around the cooling system. Refer to "Cooling and heating".

Coolant sensor – A sensor used in an engine management system, or possibly in several other systems to provide information on the temperature of the engine coolant.

Cooling fan – See Fan.

Crankcase – The area of the cylinder block below the pistons, which houses the crankshaft. Refer to "The engine".

Crankshaft – A cranked metal shaft which translates the up-and-down motion of the pistons and connecting rods into rotary motion. Refer to "The engine".

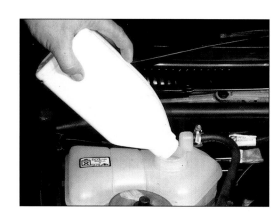

Crankshaft sensor – A sensor used in an engine management system to provide information on the position and/or speed of the crankshaft.

Cubic capacity – The total volume inside an engine which is swept by the movement of all the pistons.

CVT – Continuously Variable Transmission. An automatic transmission with no fixed gear ratios. The gear ratios are constantly varied using a system of conical pulleys and a drivebelt. Refer to "The transmission".

Cylinder – A metal tube in the engine, in which a piston slides. The cylinders may be bored directly into the cylinder block, or cylinder liners may be fitted. Refer to "The engine".

Cylinder block – The main engine casting, which houses the cylinders, crankshaft, pistons and connecting rods. Refer to "The engine".

Cylinder head – The casting at the top of the engine which houses the valves and associated components. The cylinder head is bolted to the cylinder block. Refer to "The engine".

Cylinder head gasket – The gasket which provides a seal between the cylinder head and the cylinder block.

Cylinder liner – A metal tube which fits inside the cylinder block to form the cylinder. Each cylinder liner is matched to a particular piston, and can be renewed when worn.

Damper – See Shock absorber.

Decarbonising (decoking) – Removal of all the carbon deposits from the combustion chambers, and the tops of the pistons and cylinders in an engine.

Depreciation – The reduction in value of a car as time passes.

Derv – Abbreviation for Diesel-Engines Road Vehicle. A term often used for diesel fuel.

Diagnostic light – A warning light on the instrument panel which illuminates when a fault code has been stored in an electronic control unit memory. Refer to "The engine".

Diaphragm – A flexible membrane used in some components such as brake servos. The diaphragm spring used on clutches is similar, but is made from sprung steel.

Diesel engine – An engine which relies on the heat produced when compressing air to ignite the fuel, and so doesn't need an ignition system. Diesel engines have a much higher compression ratio than petrol engines. Refer to "The engine".

Differential – A system of gears which provides drive to two wheels, but allows the wheels to turn at different speeds, for example during cornering. Refer to "The transmission".

Dipstick – A metal or plastic rod with graduated marks used to check the level of a fluid.

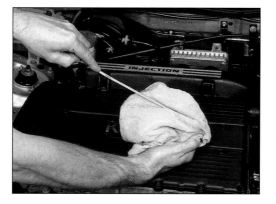

Direct injection – A type of diesel engine fuel injection system where the fuel is injected by a fuel injector directly into the combustion chamber. Refer to "The engine".

DIS – Direct Ignition System or Distributorless Ignition System. An ignition system which uses an electronic control module to replace the distributor. Refer to "The engine".

Distributor – A device used to distribute the ignition HT circuit current to the individual spark plugs. The distributor may also control the ignition timing. Refer to "The engine".

Distributor cap – A plastic cap which fits on top of the distributor. The cap contains electrodes (one for each cylinder) inside which the rotor arm rotates to distribute the HT circuit current to the correct spark plug.

DOHC – Double OverHead Camshafts. An engine with two camshafts, where one operates the inlet valves, and the other operates the exhaust valves. Allows the valves to be positioned for greater efficiency (improved flow of mixture and exhaust gases).

Drivebelt – A belt, usually made from rubber, used to transmit drive between two pulleys or sprockets. Often used to drive the camshafts (see Timing belt), and engine ancillaries. Refer to "The engine".

Driveshaft – Term used to describe a shaft which transmits drive from a differential to one wheel. Refer to "The transmission".

Drivetrain – A collective term used to describe the engine/clutch/gearbox/transmission and other components used to transmit drive to the wheels.

Drum brake – See Brake drum.

Dwell angle – A measurement relating to the ignition timing. Normally only used in relation to contact breakers in a distributor.

Earth strap – A flexible electrical connection between the battery and the car's body, or between the engine/transmission and the body to provide an electrical earth return to the battery.

EFI – Electronic Fuel Injection. See Fuel injection.

EGR – Exhaust Gas Recirculation. An emission control system which recirculates a proportion of the exhaust gases back into the engine where they are burnt with fresh mixture. Refer to "The engine".

Electrode – An electrical terminal, eg, in a spark plug or distributor cap.

Electronic control unit – A unit which receives electrical inputs from various sensors, processes the inputs, and produces electrical outputs to control one or more actuators.

Electrolyte – A solution of sulphuric acid and distilled water which conducts electrical current in a battery.

Emissions – Harmful substances (gases or particles) released into the atmosphere from a car's systems (usually the exhaust, fuel system or engine breather system). Refer to "The engine".

Emission control – A method of reducing the emissions released into the atmosphere. Various different systems are used. Refer to "The engine".

Endfloat – The axial free play of a component; for example the endfloat of the crankshaft in its bearings.

Engine management system – A system which uses an electronic control unit to control the operation of the ignition system and fuel injection system, improving engine efficiency and reducing emissions. Refer to "The engine".

EVAP – An emission control system on petrol-engined cars which stores vapour from the fuel tank and then releases it to be burnt, along with fresh mixture, by the engine. Refer to "The engine".

Excess – The part of an insurance claim paid by the insured.

Expansion tank – A container used in many car's cooling systems to collect the overflow from the cooling system as the coolant heats up and expands. Refer to "Cooling and heating".

Exhaust manifold – A device used for ducting the exhaust gases from the engine's cylinder head into the exhaust system.

Fan – Electric or engine-driven fan mounted at the front of the engine compartment and designed to cool the radiator. Refer to "Cooling and heating".

Fan belt – Another term for a drivebelt. The name arose because on older cars a drivebelt was used to drive the cooling fan. Electric cooling fans are used on most modern cars.

Fault code – An electronic code stored in the memory of an electronic control unit which gives details of a fault detected by the self-diagnostic system. A diagnostic light on the instrument panel will usually illuminate to indicate a fault. Refer to "The engine".

Fault code reader – An electronic tool used to translate fault codes into a form which indicates where the fault lies.

Feeler gauges/blades – Thin strips of metal of a measured thickness. Used to check a spark plug gap.

Final drive – Another term used to describe a differential assembly.

Firing order – The order in which the pistons in the cylinders of an engine reach their firing points.

Firing point – The instant at which the mixture in the cylinder of an engine ignites in the combustion chamber. Refer to "The engine".

Fixed caliper – A brake caliper which is rigidly fixed in position. A fixed caliper has at least two pistons, one piston to operate each brake pad. Refer to "Running gear".

Flat-engine – A form of engine in which the cylinders are opposed horizontally, usually with an equal number on each side of the crankshaft.

Flywheel – A heavy metal disc attached to one end of the crankshaft in an engine, used to smooth out the power pulses from the pistons. Refer to "The engine".

Four-stroke – A term used to describe the four operating strokes of a piston in a car engine. Refer to "The engine".

Free play – The "looseness" in a linkage, or an assembly of parts, between the initial application of force and actual movement. For example the distance the brake pedal moves before the master cylinder is actuated.

Friction disc – A metal disc with friction material attached to both sides used in a clutch assembly to progressively couple two rotating components together. Refer to "The transmission".

FSH – Full Service History. A written record which shows that a car has been serviced from new in accordance with the manufacturer's recommendations.

Fuel filter – A renewable filter which removes foreign particles from the fuel. Refer to "Fluids and filters".

Fuel injection – A method of injecting a measured amount of fuel into an engine. Used on all diesel engines, and used on most modern petrol engines in place of a carburettor. Refer to "The engine".

Fuel injection pump – A device which controls the quantity of fuel delivered to the fuel injectors in a diesel engine, and also controls the instant at which the injectors inject fuel. Refer to "The engine".

Fuel injector – A device used to inject fuel directly or indirectly into the combustion chamber in an engine. Some engines use a single fuel injector, whilst some use one fuel injector for each cylinder of the engine. Refer to "The engine".

Fuel pressure regulator – A device which controls the pressure of the fuel delivered to the fuel injectors in a petrol fuel injection engine. The pressure regulator is usually vacuum-operated by vacuum from the inlet manifold.

Fuel pump – A device which pumps fuel from the fuel tank to the fuel system.

Gasket – A compressible material used between two surfaces to give a leakproof joint.

Gearbox – A group of gears and shafts in a housing positioned between the engine and differential, used to keep a car's engine within its safe operating speed range as the speed of the car changes. Refer to "The transmission".

Glow plug – An electrical heating device fitted to a diesel engine to help the engine to start from cold, and to reduce the smoke produced immediately after start-up. Each cylinder usually has its own glow plug. Refer to "The engine".

Head gasket – A gasket fitted to provide a leakproof seal between an engine's cylinder block and cylinder head.

Heater matrix – A small radiator mounted in the engine's coolant circuit which provides hot air for the car's heating system. Hot coolant flows through the matrix, which heats the surrounding air. Refer to "Cooling and heating".

Helical gears – Gears in which the teeth are cut at an angle across the circumference of the gear to give a smoother mesh between the gears and quieter running.

Horsepower – A measurement of the power of an engine. Brake horsepower (BHP) is a measure of the power available to stop a moving body.

HT (high tension) circuit – The electrical circuit containing the high voltage used to fire the spark plugs in an ignition system. Refer to "The engine".

HT (high tension) leads – Electrical leads which carry the HT circuit voltage to the spark plugs.

Hub carrier – A component in a suspension system which carries a brake assembly and a roadwheel. Refer to "Running gear".

Hydraulic – A term used to describe the operation of a component of system by means of fluid pressure.

Hydraulic lifter (or tappet) – A valve lifter where the valve clearance is taken up hydraulically using oil pressure. This eliminates the need for valve clearance adjustment.

Hydro-pneumatic suspension – A suspension system where hydraulic units take the place of springs and (sometimes) shock absorbers in a conventional suspension system. Refer to "Running gear".

Idle speed – The running speed of an engine when the throttle is closed.

Ignition coil – An electrical coil which generates the HT circuit voltage in an ignition system. Refer to "The engine".

Ignition system – The electrical system which provides the spark to ignite the air/fuel mixture in a petrol engine. Refer to "The engine".

Ignition timing – The instant in the cylinder firing cycle at which ignition spark (provided by the spark plug) occurs in a petrol engine. The firing point is usually a few degrees of crankshaft rotation before the piston reaches the top of its stroke. Refer to "The engine".

Independent suspension – A suspension system where movement of one wheel has no effect on the movement of the other, eg, independent front suspension. Refer to "Running gear".

Indirect injection – A type of diesel engine fuel injection system where the fuel is injected by a fuel injector into a swirl chamber before entering the combustion chamber. Refer to "The engine".

Inertia reel – Automatic type of seat belt mechanism which allows the wearer to move freely in normal use, but locks when the car decelerates suddenly or the wearer moves suddenly.

Injection timing – The instant in the cylinder firing cycle at which fuel injection occurs in a diesel engine. Refer to "The engine".

Inlet manifold – A device used for ducting the air, or air/fuel mixture into the engine's cylinder head.

In-line engine – An engine in which the cylinders are positioned in a row, instead of in a vee or flat configuration.

Input shaft – The shaft which transmits drive from the clutch to the gearbox in a manual gearbox, or from the torque converter to the transmission in an automatic transmission. Refer to "The transmission".

Jump leads – Heavy electrical cables fitted with clamps to enable a car's battery to be connected to another for emergency starting. Refer to "In an emergency".

Kickdown – A device used on an automatic transmission which allows a lower gear to be selected for improved acceleration by fully depressing the accelerator pedal.

Knocking (Pinking) – A metallic noise from the engine often caused by the ignition timing being incorrect or a build-up of carbon inside the engine. The noise is due to pressure waves which cause the cylinder walls to vibrate.

Knock sensor – A sensor which senses the onset of knocking, and sends an electrical signal to the engine management system.

Lambda sensor – See Oxygen sensor.

Laminated windscreen – A windscreen which has a thin plastic layer sandwiched between two layers of toughened glass. It will not shatter or craze when hit.

Leaded petrol – 4-star petrol. Has a low amount of lead added during manufacture in addition to the natural lead found in crude oil.

Leaf spring – A suspension spring commonly used on older cars with a solid rear axle, consisting of several long curved steel plates clamped together.

Lean – A term used to describe an air/fuel mixture containing less than the optimum amount of fuel.

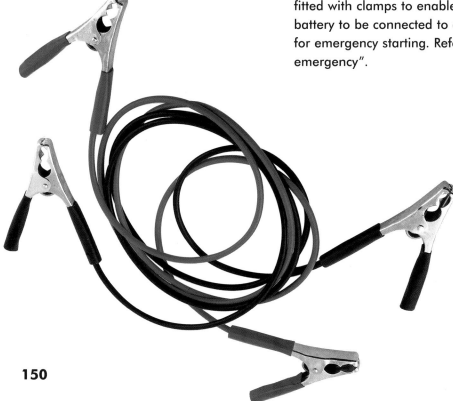

LHM – A special type of mineral-based hydraulic fluid used in Citroën hydraulic systems. Refer to "Fluids and filters".

Locknut – a nut used to lock an adjustment nut, or another threaded component in place.

Lockwasher – A washer designed to prevent a nut or bolt from working loose.

LPG – Liquefied Petroleum Gas. A mixture of liquefied petroleum gases, such as propane and butane, which are obtained from crude oil. Used in some engines as an alternative to petrol and diesel fuel. Refer to "All about fuel".

MacPherson strut – An independent suspension component, which combines a coil spring and a shock absorber so that the swivelling, springing and shock absorbing for a wheel is carried out by a single assembly. Refer to "Running gear".

MAP sensor – Manifold Absolute Pressure sensor. A sensor which measures the pressure in the inlet manifold of a petrol engine, and sends an electrical signal to the engine management system.

Mass airflow sensor – A sensor used in an engine management system to measure the mass of air being sucked into the engine.

Master cylinder – A cylinder containing a piston and hydraulic fluid, directly coupled to a foot pedal (or brake servo). Used for transmitting fluid pressure to the brake or clutch operating mechanisms. Refer to "Running gear".

Mixture – The air/fuel mixture burnt by an engine to produce power. In a petrol engine, the optimum ratio of fuel to air for complete combustion is 14.7:1. Refer to "The engine".

Multi-point fuel injection – A fuel injection system which has one fuel injector for each cylinder of the engine. Refer to "The engine".

Multi-valve – An engine with more than two valves per cylinder. Usually four valves per cylinder (2 inlet and 2 exhaust valves), or sometimes three valves per cylinder (2 inlet valves and 1 exhaust valve).

NOx – Oxides of Nitrogen. Toxic emissions found in the exhaust gases of petrol and diesel engines. Refer to "The engine".

OBD – On-Board Diagnostics. A system which monitors the operation of the engine management system and records a fault code if any fault occurs in the system which may affect the emissions. Refer to "The engine".

Octane rating – A scale rating for grading petrol. The higher the octane number, the more energy a given amount of petrol will produce when it's burnt by the engine.

OHC – OverHead Camshaft. An engine layout where the camshaft is mounted above the valves. Because the camshaft operates the valves directly (via the valve gear), an OHC engine is more efficient than an OHV engine.

OHV – OverHead Valve. An engine layout where the valves are located in the cylinder head, but the valve gear is operated by pushrods from a camshaft located lower in the cylinder block.

Oil cooler – A small radiator fitted in the engine oil circuit, positioned in a cooling airflow to cool the oil. Often used on diesel engines and high-performance petrol engines.

Oil filter – A renewable filter which removes foreign particles from the engine oil. Refer to "Fluids and filters".

Open-loop – A term for an emission control system using a catalytic converter where the catalytic converter operates independently from the fuel system. Refer to "The engine".

O-ring – A type of sealing ring made of rubber. An O-ring is usually clamped between two surfaces (often into a groove) to provide a seal.

Oxygen sensor (lambda sensor) – Provides information on the amount of oxygen present in the exhaust gases. Used in a closed-loop catalytic converter system to enable the engine management system to control the air/fuel mixture. Refer to "The engine".

PAS – See Power steering.

Pinion – A term for a gear with a small number of teeth, which meshes with a gear having a larger number of teeth.

Pinking – See Knocking.

Piston – Cylindrical component which slides in a close-fitting cylinder. The pistons in an engine compress the air/fuel mixture, transmits power to the crankshaft via the connecting rods, and push the burnt gases out through the exhaust valves. Refer to "The engine".

Piston ring – A hardened metal ring which is a spring-fit in a groove running around a piston, to ensure a gas-tight seal between the piston and the cylinder wall.

Plug – See Spark plug.

Points – See Contact breaker.

Power Assisted Steering (PAS) – A system which uses hydraulic pressure to provide assistance when the drive turns the steering wheel.

Pre-ignition – See Knocking.

Pressure cap – Acts as a cooling system safety valve by venting steam or hot coolant if the pressure rises above a certain level. Also acts as a vacuum relief valve to stop a vacuum forming in the system as it cools. Refer to "Cooling and heating".

Propeller shaft – The shaft which transmits drive from the manual gearbox or automatic transmission to the differential in a front-engined, rear-wheel-drive or four-wheel-drive car. Refer to "The transmission".

Pulse air – An emission control system which introduces fresh air into the exhaust manifold through tubes, to raise the temperature of the exhaust gases. This in turn causes the catalytic converter to warm up more quickly. Refer to "The engine".

Rack-and-pinion – A form of steering mechanism where the steering wheel moves a pinion gear, which in turn moves a toothed rack connected to the roadwheels.

Radial tyre – A tyre where the fabric material plies (under the tread) are arranged at right-angles to the circumference of the tyre.

Radiator – A cooling device, located in a cooling airflow, through which a hot liquid is passed,. A radiator is made up of fine tubes and fins to allow rapid cooling of the liquid inside. Refer to "Cooling and heating".

Rebore – The process of enlarging the cylinder bores very accurately so that new, larger pistons can be fitted to overcome wear in the engine. Not normally necessary unless the engine has covered a very high mileage.

Refrigerant – The substance used to absorb heat in an air conditioning system. The refrigerant is changed from a gas to a liquid and vice versa during the air conditioning process.

Regrind – The process of reducing the diameter of the bearing surfaces on a crankshaft or camshaft so that new, smaller diameter bearings can be fitted to overcome wear in the engine. Not normally required unless the engine has covered a very high mileage.

Release arm or lever – The device which transmits the movement of the clutch pedal to the clutch release bearing. Refer to "The transmission".

Release bearing – A bearing which is used to operate a clutch. The bearing is used to allow for the fact that the release arm (or lever) moves laterally, and the clutch components are rotating. Refer to "The transmission".

Rich – A term used to describe an air/fuel mixture containing more than the optimum amount of fuel.

Rocker arm – A lever which rocks on a central pivot, with one end moved up and down by the camshaft, and the other end operating a valve.

Rotary (Wankel) engine – An engine which has a triangular shaped rotor instead of the pistons used in a conventional engine. The rotor rotates in a housing shaped like a broad figure-of-eight. Very few cars have this type of engine.

Rotor arm – A rotating arm in a distributor, which distributes the HT circuit voltage to correct spark plug. An electrode on the rotor arm distributes the voltage to electrodes in the distributor cap, which are connected to the HT leads.

Running-on – A tendency for the engine to keep on running after the ignition has been switched off. Often caused by incorrect ignition timing, the wrong grade of fuel, or a poorly maintained engine.

Screenwash – See Washer fluid.

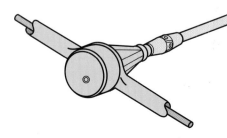

Self-diagnostic system – A system which monitors the operation of an electronically-controlled system, and stores a fault code in the system electronic control unit memory if a fault is detected.

Semi-trailing arm – A common form of independent rear suspension.

Servo – A device for increasing the normal effort applied to a control.

Shim – A thin spacer, often used to adjust the clearance between two parts; for example shims located under bucket tappets control the valve clearances.

Shock absorber – A device used to damp out the up-and-down movement of the suspension when the car hits a bump in the road. Refer to "Running gear".

Single-point fuel injection – A fuel injection system which has a single fuel injector. Refer to "The engine".

Slave cylinder – A cylinder containing a piston and hydraulic fluid, which receives hydraulic fluid pressure from a master cylinder, via a pipe, and uses movement of the piston to operate a mechanism.

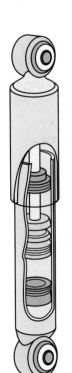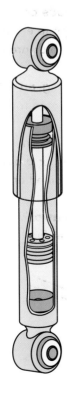

Sliding caliper – A brake caliper which slides sideways in order to clamp the brake pads against the brake disc. A sliding caliper needs only one piston to operates both brake pads. Refer to "Running gear".

SOHC – Single OverHead Camshaft. An OHC engine with a single camshaft.

Solid rear axle – A rear suspension system where movement of one roadwheel directly affects the movement of the other.

Spark plug – A device which provides the spark in a petrol engine's combustion chamber in order to ignite the air/fuel mixture. The HT circuit voltage jumps between two electrodes on the spark plug, creating a spark. Refer to "The engine".

Spark plug gap – The air gap between the electrodes on a spark plug. Refer to "The engine".

Starter motor – An electric motor used to start the engine. A pinion gear on the starter motor, engages with a large gear on the engine's flywheel, which turns the crankshaft. Refer to "Electrical things".

Steering gear – A general term used to describe the steering components. Usually refers to a steering rack-and-pinion assembly. Refer to "Running gear".

Steering rack – See Rack-and-pinion.

Stroke – The total distance travelled by a single piston in a cylinder when it moves from the bottom to the top of its movement.

Strut – See MacPherson strut.

Stub axle – A short axle which carries one roadwheel.

Subframe – A small frame mounted underneath a car's body which carries the suspension and/or drivetrain assemblies.

Sump – The main reservoir for the engine oil.

Supercharger – A device which uses an engine-driven turbine (usually driven from the crankshaft) to drive a compressor which forces air into the engine. This provides better air/fuel mixture flow into the engine and therefore more power.

Swirl chamber – A device used in a diesel engine to swirl the fuel around to mix it with air before the mixture passes to the combustion chamber. Refer to "The engine".

Suppressor – A device used to reduce or eliminate electrical interference caused by the ignition system or other electrical components.

Suspension – A general term used to describe the system which insulates a car's body from the roadwheels, and keeps all four roadwheels in contact with the road surface. Refer to "Running gear".

Synchromesh – A device used in a manual gearbox to synchronise the speed of two gears to produce smooth quiet engagement of the gears. Refer to "The transmission".

Tachometer (rev. counter) – Indicates engine speed in revolutions per minute.

Tappet – See Cam follower.

Tappet adjustment – See Valve clearance.

Thermostat – A device which aids engine warm-up by preventing the coolant from flowing through the radiator, until a pre-determined temperature is reached. The thermostat then regulates the temperature of the coolant. Refer to "Cooling and heating".

Throttle position sensor – A sensor used in an engine management system to provide information on the position of the throttle valve.

Throttle valve – A flap valve controlled by the accelerator pedal, located between the air cleaner and the inlet manifold, which controls the amount of air entering the engine.

Tie-rod (track-rod) – See Track-rod.

Timing belt (cam belt) – Fabric or rubber toothed drivebelt, used to transmit drive from the crankshaft to the camshaft(s). Refer to "The engine".

Timing chain – Metal flexible link chain which engages with sprockets, used to transmit drive from the crankshaft to the camshaft(s). Refer to "The engine".

Timing marks – Marks normally found on the crankshaft pulley or the flywheel, and the camshaft sprocket(s). Used to set the engine's ignition firing point with respect to a particular piston.

Toe-in/toe-out – The angle at which the front wheels point inwards or outwards from the straight-ahead position when the steering is positioned straight-ahead. Toe-in is when the front edges of the wheels point inwards.

Top Dead Centre (TDC) – The exact point at which a piston is at the top of its stroke.

Torque – The turning force generated by a rotating component.

Torque wrench – A tool used to tighten fasteners to a prescribed tightness.

Torque converter – A coupling used in an automatic transmission between the engine's flywheel and the transmission. The driving torque is transmitted through oil inside the torque converter. Refer to "The transmission".

Torsion bar – A metal bar which twists about its own axis. Used in some suspension systems.

Torx – A type of fastener, usually a screw or bolt, which needs a specially-shaped (Torx) socket or key to remove and refit it. Torx fasteners come in various standard sizes.

Toughened windscreen – A windscreen which when hit will shatter in a particular way to produce blunt-edged fragments, or will craze but remain intact.

Track-rod (tie-rod) – A metal rod which connects the steering gear to a hub carrier. The track-rods move the front wheels when the steering wheel is turned. Refer to "Running gear".

Trailing arm – A form of independent suspension where the roadwheel is attached to a pivoting arm, with the wheel mounted to the rear of the pivot.

Transaxle – A combined gearbox/ differential assembly from which two driveshafts transmit the drive to the wheels.

Transmission – A general term used to describe some or all of the drivetrain components excluding the engine. Commonly used to describe automatic gearboxes. Refer to "The transmission".

Turbocharger – A device which uses a turbine driven by the engine exhaust gases to drive a compressor which forces air into the engine. This provides better air/fuel mixture flow into the engine and therefore more power.

Twin-cam – Abbreviation for twin overhead camshafts – see DOHC.

Universal joint – A joint that can move in any direction whilst transmitting torque. Used in propeller shafts and some driveshafts. Not suitable for some uses because the input and output shaft speeds are not always the same for all angles of the joint.

Unleaded petrol – Petrol which had no lead added during manufacture, but still has the natural lead content of crude oil.

Vacuum pump – A pump driven by the engine which creates vacuum to operate the brake servo on a diesel engine.

Valves – A device which opens of closes to stop or allow gas or fluid flow.

Valve clearance – The clearance between the top of a valve and the camshaft, necessary to allow the valve to close fully, and to allow for expansion of the valvegear components. Often adjusted by adjusting the clearance between the tappet and camshaft.

Valve gear – A general term for the components which are acted on by a camshaft to operate the valves.

Valve lifter – See Cam follower.

16-valve – A term used to describe a four-cylinder engine with four valves per cylinder, usually two exhaust and two inlet valves. Gives improved efficiency due to improved air/fuel mixture and exhaust gas flow in the combustion chambers.

Vee-engine – An engine design in which the cylinders are arranged in two rows forming a "V" when viewed from one end. For example a V8 has two rows of four cylinders each.

Voltage regulator – A device which regulates the output of the alternator.

Voluntary excess – see Excess.

Wankel engine – See Rotary engine.

Washer fluid – The water used to wash the windscreen, etc. Often with a detergent additive to improve cleaning and resist freezing.

Washer jet – The nozzle which directs washer fluid onto the windscreen.

Water (coolant) pump – See Coolant pump.

Wheel alignment – The process of checking the toe-in/toe-out, and sometimes the camber and castor angles of the wheels. On most cars, only the toe-in/toe-out can be adjusted. Incorrect wheel alignment can cause tyre wear and poor handling.

Wheel balancing – The process of adding small weights to the rim of a wheel so that there are no out-of-balance forces when the wheel rotates.

Wheel cylinder – A slave cylinder used to operate the brake shoes in a drum brake. Refer to "Running gear".

Wheel brace – The tool used to slacken the nuts or bolts holding the wheel on the car.

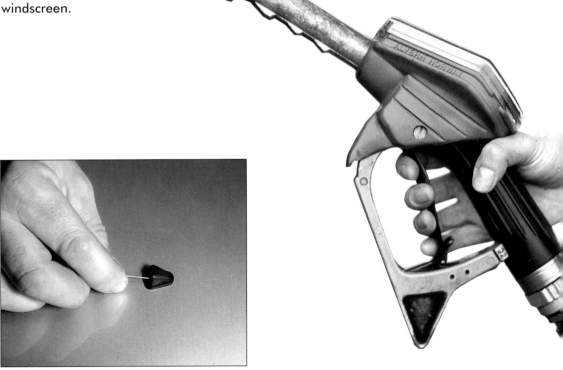

Index

Acknowledgements

The author and publishers would like to thank the following:

Loders of Yeovil, Somerset
Sedna Service Station, Queen Camel, Somerset
Richard White's Garage, Sparkford, Somerset
Britax Excelsior Limited, Andover, Hampshire

Author:	Steve Rendle
Editor:	Ian Barnes
Proof-reader:	Dave Rankin
Photographs:	Andrew Morland & Steve Rendle
Illustrations:	Steve Tanswell, Paul Tanswell & Matthew Marke
Cover design:	Graham Webb
Page Make-up:	Jill Gough
Project Manager:	Louise McIntyre
Production Manager:	Kevin Perrett

© Haynes Publishing 1999
Reprinted 2000

Published by: Haynes Publishing, Sparkford, nr Yeovil, Somerset BA22 7JJ

British Library Cataloguing-in-Publication Data:
A catalogue record for this book is available from the British Library.

ISBN 1 85960 488 9

Printed in France by Pollina

While every effort is taken to ensure the accuracy of the information given in this book, no liability can be accepted by the author or the publisher for any loss, damage or injury caused by errors in, or omissions from, the information given.